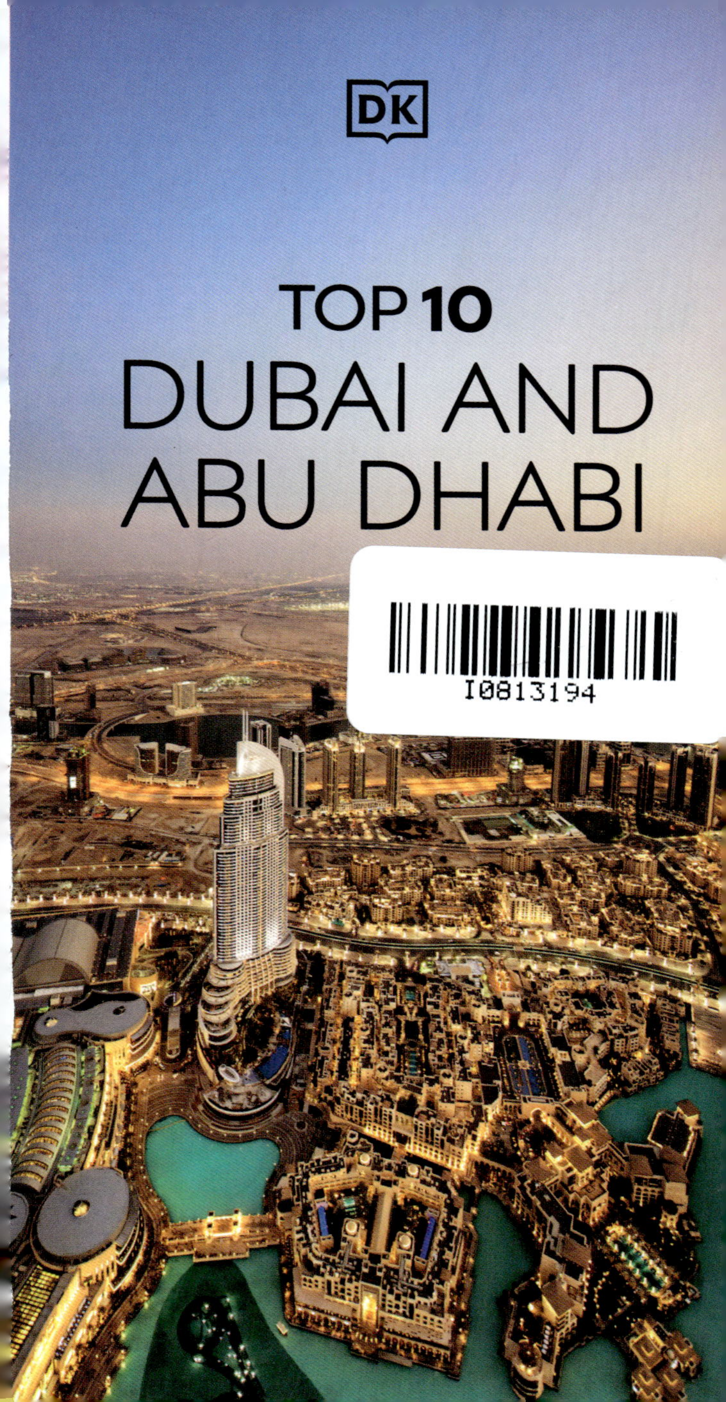
DK
TOP 10
DUBAI AND
ABU DHABI
I0813194

CONTENTS

42

Top 10 of Everything

60

Area by Area

104

Streetsmart

DUBAI AND ABU DHABI

INTRODUCING

The Palm Jumeirah

WELCOME TO

DUBAI AND ABU DHABI

The world's only "seven-star" hotel, ski slopes in malls, artificial islands filled with luxury resorts and theme parks. It can only be the UAE. Don't want to miss a thing? With Top 10 Dubai and Abu Dhabi, you'll enjoy the very best these emirates have to offer.

The endless sunshine, miles of coastline and iconic landmarks have all made the UAE a holiday hotspot for millions of visitors. If it's the tallest, the biggest or the fastest in the world, it's probably here. In one day in Dubai, you can ride the tallest ferris wheel on the planet, Ain Dubai, and tour the tallest building in the world, Burj Khalifa, before a swim in

Driving the dunes near Dubai

the world's highest infinity pool, Aura Skypool. If that's not enough superlatives, try dining at one of Dubai's 19 Michelin-starred restaurants or spend a day wandering the more than 1,000 shops inside the Dubai Mall.

And just a short journey down the coast is Abu Dhabi, the capital of the UAE. Not content to live in Dubai's shadow, Abu Dhabi is home to its own first-class highlights, from the fastest roller coaster in the world at Ferrari World to the opulent splendour of the Sheikh Zayed Grand Mosque. There's incredible shopping to be had amid the towering sights, including at the busy souks of Al Mina port and the luxury stores at Marina Mall.

But these two emirates are more than architecture, luxury dining and world-class shopping – here you'll find some of the finest beaches in the Middle East and historical sites such as Dubai Creek, filled with traditional *abra* boats. And in the evening, tours into the desert allow you to explore sweeping sand dunes and enjoy a feast under the stars.

So, where to start? With Top 10 Dubai and Abu Dhabi, of course. This pocket-sized guide gets to the heart of these two emirates with simple lists of 10, expert local knowledge and comprehensive maps, helping you turn an ordinary trip into an extraordinary one.

THE STORY OF **DUBAI AND ABU DHABI**

From its origin as a land of pearl divers and desert nomads, the UAE has played a big role in shaping the region. At the heart of this journey are Dubai and Abu Dhabi, two emirates that have carved out unique yet complementary identities. Here's the story of how they came to be.

The First Settlers

The history of Dubai and Abu Dhabi can be traced back thousands of years, with archaeological evidence suggesting Abu Dhabi was inhabited by 6000 BCE. Early settlers of the Palaeolithic Age were primarily fishermen, nomadic herders and date farmers, occupations that endured throughout the ages. A few thousand years later, around 3000 BCE, the area around modern Dubai, once a mangrove swamp, was also settled, again by herders and farmers of the Umm Al Nar people. Settlements in both future emirates remained small, but during the Roman Empire, Abu Dhabi became a key entrepôt in the Arabian Peninsula, linking people with goods from Europe, Mesopotamia and India. Unfortunately, the paucity of records means there is little more we know about this period, as well as the millennium that followed.

Embracing Islam

Historical evidence resurfaces in the 7th century CE, around the time of the spread of Islam across the Middle East. This coincided with the military conquest by the Umayyad Caliphate, who established the first Muslim Empire. Envoys from the Prophet Muhammad were sent to various local peoples, inviting them to embrace Islam. The religion quickly took root, influencing governance, trade and daily life. Its arrival marked a profound transformation in the region's identity, uniting disparate

Trading vessels moored along the coast of Dubai

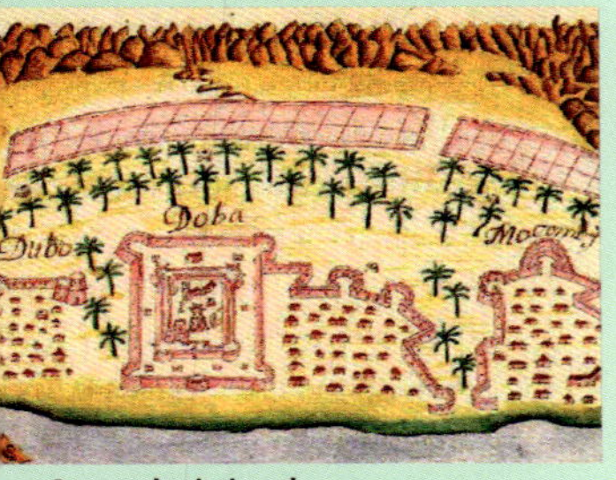

A map depicting the Portuguese fort of Doba

peoples under a common faith. Mosques were built and trade flourished as the region became integrated into the broader Islamic Empire that stretched from the Iberian Peninsula to India.

European Invasions

The prosperity of the Arabian Peninsula continued under the Abbasid Caliphate, who had overthrown the Umayyad Caliphate in the 8th century. However, after their empire was smashed by the Mongols in the 13th century, the region receded into a backwater. That changed in the 16th century with the arrival of the Portuguese, who conquered much of the Middle East, establishing direct rule over the coastal regions and creating a near trade monopoly. Their decline in the mid-1600s paved the way for Dutch and British rule over the following centuries. All these European powers came here nominally to secure trade against local pirates, but the real attraction was the local pearl economy.

It was during this time that the cities of Dubai and Abu Dhabi started to take shape – Abu Dhabi in 1761, after the Bani Yas tribe discovered freshwater on Abu Dhabi island, and Dubai by 1799, according to documents. This Dubai settlement was initially dependent on Abu Dhabi, but this changed in 1830 when a branch of the Bani Yas rulers left Abu Dhabi and took power in Dubai. In doing so, they created the Al Maktoum dynasty that rules Dubai to this day.

Moments in History

6000 BCE

The modern area of Abu Dhabi is settled by fishermen, herders and date farmers.

3000 BCE

The Bronze Age Umm Al Nar civilization emerges, known for its trade and distinctive circular tombs.

7th century CE

Following the Umayyad Caliphate conquest, Islam spreads across the region, with the Prophet Muhammad's teachings being shared in the Qur'an.

1095

A place called Dubai is first mentioned in the *Book of Geography* by Andalusian-Arab geographer Abu Abdullah Al Bakri.

1498

The first European explorers arrive in the Gulf in the form of Portuguese sailors and traders. They are followed by the Dutch and the British.

1820
A number of local sheikhs sign the first of several 19th-century treaties with Britain, beginning the Trucial States era.

1958
Oil is first discovered in Abu Dhabi, soon to be followed by Dubai less than a decade later, reshaping the region's economic future.

1971
The United Arab Emirates is officially formed as a country with six emirates; Ras Al Khaimah joins in 1972.

2010
Large-scale investment across Dubai leads to the construction of the Burj Khalifa, the world's tallest building.

2021
The UAE becomes the first Middle East country to host a World Expo, one of the first global gatherings after the COVID-19 pandemic.

Trucial States

By the 19th century, the Arabian Peninsula had been divided up into independent sheikhdoms. These rulers were powerful in their own kingdom, but true power in the region lay with Britain. Their military had already stamped out piracy and subdued local threats. Between 1820 and 1853, they cemented power through a series of peace treaties with local rulers, through which these sheikhdoms became known as the Trucial States. These treaties increased British authority over the region but allowed each sheikh to retain control over their internal affairs. A further agreement in 1892 gave the region British military protection, but forbade the sheikhs from entering into partnerships with any country without the permission of the UK.

At the same time, the region was experiencing an economic boom, driven by the pearling industry. The abundant pearls off the Arabian coast had been the lifeblood of the local economy for centuries, but high demand during the 19th and early 20th centuries allowed the industry to flourish and many to grow rich. But this proved short-lived.

First ruler of the UAE, Sheikh Zayed bin Sultan Al Nahyan

The skyline of Downtown Dubai

The combined effect of the Great Depression and the invention of the cultured pearl in Japan led prices to fall and the industry to collapse.

The Birth of the UAE

After this decline, the emirates were little more than a series of sparsely populated trading hubs. But that all changed in 1958 with the discovery of oil in Abu Dhabi. The first barrel of "black gold" was exported in 1962 and four years later, Dubai also struck oil. These discoveries marked the start of a dramatic economic transformation that was soon followed by equally seismic political change. In January 1968, the UK announced it would end its relationship with the emirate states by 1971. Within a month, the Trucial States (led by Dubai and Abu Dhabi), Bahrain and Qatar had agreed to form a federation of emirates. Although Bahrain and Qatar withdrew later in the year, the remaining sheikhdoms held together and on 2 December 1971, Abu Dhabi, Dubai, Sharjah, Umm Al Quwain, Fujairah and Ajman formed the United Arab Emirates, with Sheikh Zayed bin Sultan Al Nahyan of Abu Dhabi named president. The birth of the UAE coincided with a great economic boom, triggered by soaring oil prices in the mid-1970s. Thanks to this, the country's GDP surpassed $40 billion USD in 1980.

Dubai and Abu Dhabi Today

The economy continued its upward trajectory over the following decades, with the newfound wealth strategically reinvested into funding large-scale developments in infrastructure, education, healthcare and industry. Abu Dhabi and Dubai quickly became the most powerful emirates; global centres of politics, finance and trade. Concurrent to conquering these arenas, the 21st century has seen both emirates diversify and establish themselves as world-class tourism and business destinations. Dubai, in particular, is now synonymous with luxury and innovation through landmark developments such as the "seven-star" Burj Al Arab hotel, Palm Jumeirah and Burj Khalifa. Meanwhile, Abu Dhabi has focused on cultural investments, opening the Louvre Abu Dhabi as the first of many world-class galleries and museums. With their futuristic skylines, ultramodern infrastructure and commitment to first-class service, Dubai and Abu Dhabi have successfully positioned themselves as premier destinations for years to come.

TOP 10 EXPERIENCES

Planning the perfect trip to Dubai and Abu Dhabi? Whether you're visiting for the first time or making a return trip, there are some things you simply shouldn't miss out on. To make the most of your time – and to enjoy the very best these cities have to offer – be sure to add these experiences to your list.

1 Shop in the souks

Leave modern Dubai behind and travel back in time on a trip through the labyrinthine alleys of the historic souks *(p34)*. Here you can shop for fragrant frankincense, pungent spices, intricate jewellery and Arabian textiles. Sharpen your haggling skills for the full, immersive market experience.

2 Swim under the stars

After-dark dips are quite possibly the best way to cool off in Dubai and Abu Dhabi. The waters around both emirates are still warm but the risk of sunburn is gone. Dubai's three designated night beaches, Jumeirah 2, Jumeirah 3 and Umm Suqeim 1, are perfect for a romantic moonlit swim.

3 Hike in Hatta

Nestled in the Hajar Mountains, away from the skyscrapers of Dubai, Hatta *(p58)* is an adventure-lover's haven, offering scenic trails and serene pools to swim in. Snap a selfie at the Hollywood-style Hatta sign before kayaking or mountain biking through this stunning moonlike landscape.

4 Live the luxury lifestyle

The UAE is a byword for opulence and you can experience luxury in all its forms. Go window-shopping along Fashion Avenue in Dubai Mall *(p77)*, hire a high-end car to cruise the streets in, taste the finest Michelin-starred food at Indego by Vineet *(p91)* or spend the night at a five-star hotel *(p114)*.

5 Admire the architecture

Can you really say you've been to the UAE if you haven't visited its architectural titans? The emirates are filled with many modern marvels such as the sail-shaped Jumeirah Burj Al Arab *(p30)*, the unusual Dubai Frame and the record-breaking Burj Khalifa *(p22)*.

6 Go on a desert safari

For a taste of Bedouin life, head inland to the sand dunes. Half-day desert safaris *(p40)* tick a lot of boxes, including thrilling 4WD dune-bashing drives, sandboarding, henna hand painting and a delicious Arabian buffet beneath the stars.

7 Eat an authentic shawarma

With its juicy meat, pickles, garlicky sauce and soft Arabian bread, shawarma is the UAE's national street food. It's found everywhere from stalls to cafés, and Aroos Damascus *(p66)* has versions you'll dream about long after leaving.

8 Party at a beach club

Soak up the sun (and the vibes) at one of the UAE's stylish beach clubs. Enjoy the laid-back lounge at the Cove Beach Club *(p87)*, experience luxury at the clubs along J1 Beach *(j1beach.com)* or enjoy a relaxed drink while you look out over the sea at Cabana 9 *(p102)*.

9 Take a boat trip

Historically this was an area dominated by boats, from sea traders to pirates. Re-create historical journeys by crossing Dubai Creek on an *abra*, jump in a kayak and glide through Abu Dhabi's mangroves *(p100)* or indulge in opulence and hire your own yacht.

10 Feel the need for speed

This is the home of speed in the Middle East. Major events are held at the Dubai Autodrome *(p46)* and the Yas Marina Circuit *(p39)*, home to F1's Abu Dhabi Grand Prix. Experience the speed yourself at Ferrari World *(p38)*, which has the fastest roller coaster in the world.

ITINERARIES

Ascending the Burj Khalifa, wandering the souks, admiring the Sheikh Zayed Grand Mosque: there's a lot to see and do in Dubai and Abu Dhabi. With places to eat, drink or shop, these itineraries offer ways to spend 2 days and 4 days in the UAE.

2 DAYS IN DUBAI

Day 1

Morning

Start your Dubai adventure in Jumeirah with breakfast at 21 Grams *(21grams.me)*, a charming Balkan bistro that serves up hearty dishes featuring its signature filo pies. Pair the cheese and spinach *burek* with a coffee for an energizing start to your day. After you've eaten, catch a cab or the 8 bus towards J1 Beach *(p13)*, a glamorous shoreline development of luxury beach clubs. Spend the morning lounging by the pool at the chic Bâoli Dubai *(baoli-restaurant.com/beachclub.html)*, or at Sirene Beach by Gaia *(sirenebeach.com)*, where Mediterranean flare meets soft Arabian sands. Leave the sea and sun and head indoors at Sirene for a Greek-inspired lunch where dishes are paired with the fresh catch of the day.

SHOP
The condiments at the Spice Souk *(p64)* make great souvenirs. Shop for saffron, sumac (a tangy red spice) and *za'atar* (a fragrant blend of thyme, sesame seeds and salt).

Afternoon

Satiated, take a taxi and step back in time on a visit to Old Dubai. Ride across Dubai Creek *(p24)* on a traditional *abra* *(p107)*, a wooden boat that has ferried passengers for centuries. Disembark at Deira Abra Station and stroll through

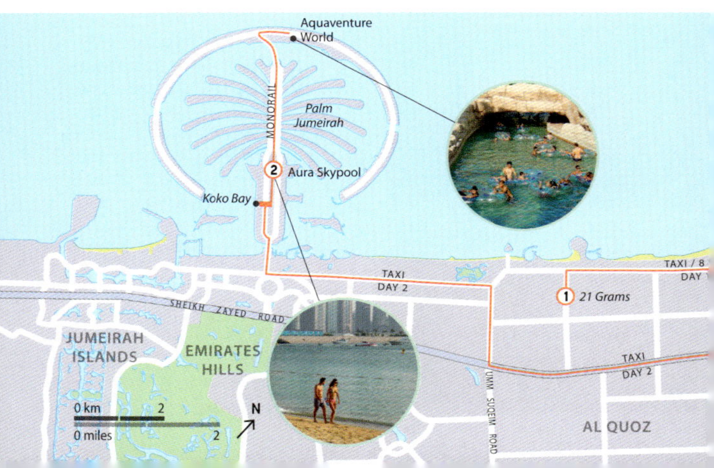

Enjoying sublime views from Aura Skypool

the scent-packed Spice Souk *(p64)*, and maybe buy a new fragrance or spice. Return across the creek for an Emirati dinner at Al Fanar *(p73)*, which specializes in the flavours of Old Dubai. Try the lamb and rice *machboos (p50)*, a dish reminiscent of a biryani.

Day 2

Morning

Begin the day with a sky-high swim at Aura Skypool *(auraskypool.com)*, the world's highest 360-degree infinity pool. Enjoy its panoramic views of the Palm Jumeirah *(p86)* before poolside yoga and a colourful breakfast bowl from Aura's restaurant. Then, hop on the Palm monorail *(p89)* and continue the aquatic theme at Aquaventure World *(p86)* at Atlantis, The Palm. See if you're brave enough to slide down the record-breaking Leap of Faith.

Afternoon

After a thrilling morning, head back along the monorail and relax at Koko Bay *(kokobay.co)*, a beachfront restaurant on West Beach. Dine on sushi rolls, seafood platters and tropical cocktails, all while sinking your toes in the sand. Take a taxi to reach your final stops in Downtown Dubai. Admire the Dubai Fountain show *(p75)* outside the Dubai Mall *(p77)*, then head inside and stroll through the mall itself, shopping at its more than 1,000 shops or watching the skiers shred powder at Ski Dubai *(p81)*. When you're ready for dinner, immerse yourself in a multi-sensory dining experience at Krasota *(krasota.art)*, where art, storytelling and gastronomy collide in a theatrical setting.

VIEW
The *Wings of Mexico* by Jorge Marín *(p23)*, a bronze sculpture of angel wings, invites passersby to step between them and create their own "flying" moment with Burj Khalifa as a backdrop.

4 DAYS IN DUBAI AND ABU DHABI

Day 1

Start your four-day trip with a beach-front breakfast at the bright, all-day eatery Eggspectation *(eggspectation.ae)* in JBR *(p32)*. Stroll down the shore to jump into the world's largest inflatable water park, AquaFun Dubai Water park *(p87)*. Tackle the slides, monkey bars and balance beams on the slippery assault course. After working up an appetite, stroll across the bridge to Bluewaters Island *(p87)* for lunch at The Blue Door in Delano Dubai *(delanohotels.com)*. Dig into Mediterranean-inspired dishes and freshly made cocktails in a stylish, laid-back setting. Afterwards, take a spin on nearby Ain Dubai *(p32)*, the world's tallest ferris wheel. As evening falls, dress up for a modern European dinner at City Social by Jason Atherton *(p91)*, a convivial dining spot on the 43rd floor of Grosvenor House Dubai.

EAT

Don't leave Dubai without sampling Trèsind *(p91)* delicious slow-cooked kebab *scarpetta*, a dish served up in a sizzling pan with a rich gravy designed to be mopped up with toasted sourdough. Magnificent.

Crossing the pedestrian bridge to Bluewaters Island, Dubai

Day 2

Indulge in a grand Dubai buffet breakfast at your nearest five-star hotel, and then head to the landmark Jumeirah Burj Al Arab *(p30)* to take a butler-led tour of the grand suites. Stick around for an early lunch at the hotel's Arabian restaurant Al Iwan, where you can sample local cuisine in a palatial setting. After lunch, amble along the vibrant Kite Beach *(p49)*. If you're up for it, take a fun kitesurfing lesson. Then, hop in a taxi to Alserkal Avenue *(p83)* to see the best of Dubai's contemporary art scene, where galleries showcase cutting-edge art, photography and installations by regional and international artists. Stay in the area for the evening and see a film at Cinema Akil *(cinemaakil.com)*,

Dubai's only independent arthouse cinema, complemented by Indian comfort food at the next-door Project Chaiwala *(projectchaiwala.com)*.

Day 3

In the morning, take a taxi or the E101 bus from Dubai to the UAE's capital, Abu Dhabi. Head to Al Mrzab Traditional Restaurant *(2 666 2333)* for an Emirati breakfast of *chebab* pancakes, and *balaleet (p50)*. Then, take the 54 bus eastwards to Mangrove National Park *(p100)* to kayak through the lush waterways and submerged forests. For lunch, head south to enjoy Michelin-starred Emirati cuisine at Earth *(earth.ae)*. After, walk 25 minutes north and visit the majestic Sheikh Zayed Grand Mosque *(p36)*, a masterpiece of Islamic architecture. Take time to admire its 82 domes and many intricate mosaics, before checking into your hotel. In the evening, embark on a desert safari *(p40)* with a 4WD excursion into the dunes, followed by a Bedouin-style dinner of meats and sweets under the stars.

Kayaking in Mangrove National Park, Abu Dhabi

Day 4

For your final morning, head straight to the Louvre Abu Dhabi *(p101)*, an architectural marvel designed by Jean Nouvel. Grab breakfast at the museum café then wander through the galleries that house priceless masterpieces from Leonardo to Van Gogh. After a couple of hours here, take the 187 bus towards the theme parks of Yas Island *(p38)*. Hold on tight for high-speed thrills at Ferrari World *(p38)*, home to the world's fastest roller coaster, and then cool off at Yas Waterworld *(p48)*, packed with 45 waterslides. Grab a quick lunch at one of the park's many eateries before taking a rest by the pool. End your trip with an opulent soirée at Emirates Palace *(p117)*, Abu Dhabi's most luxurious hotel, reachable by taxi. Dine at Hakkasan Abu Dhabi *(p97)*, where Cantonese fine dining is served in a lively club-like setting and the signature dim sum platters are adorned in gold leaf.

TOP 10 HIGHLIGHTS

Sheikh Zayed Mosque

EXPLORE THE **HIGHLIGHTS**

There are some sights in Dubai and Abu Dhabi you simply shouldn't miss, and it's these attractions that make the Top 10. Discover what makes each one a must-see on the following pages.

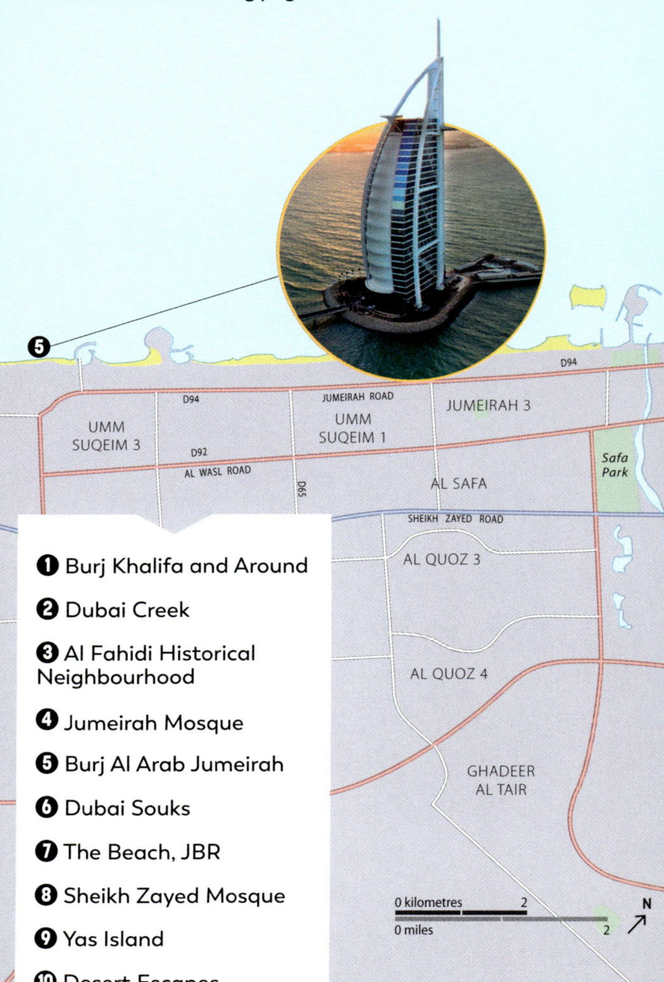

1. Burj Khalifa and Around
2. Dubai Creek
3. Al Fahidi Historical Neighbourhood
4. Jumeirah Mosque
5. Burj Al Arab Jumeirah
6. Dubai Souks
7. The Beach, JBR
8. Sheikh Zayed Mosque
9. Yas Island
10. Desert Escapes

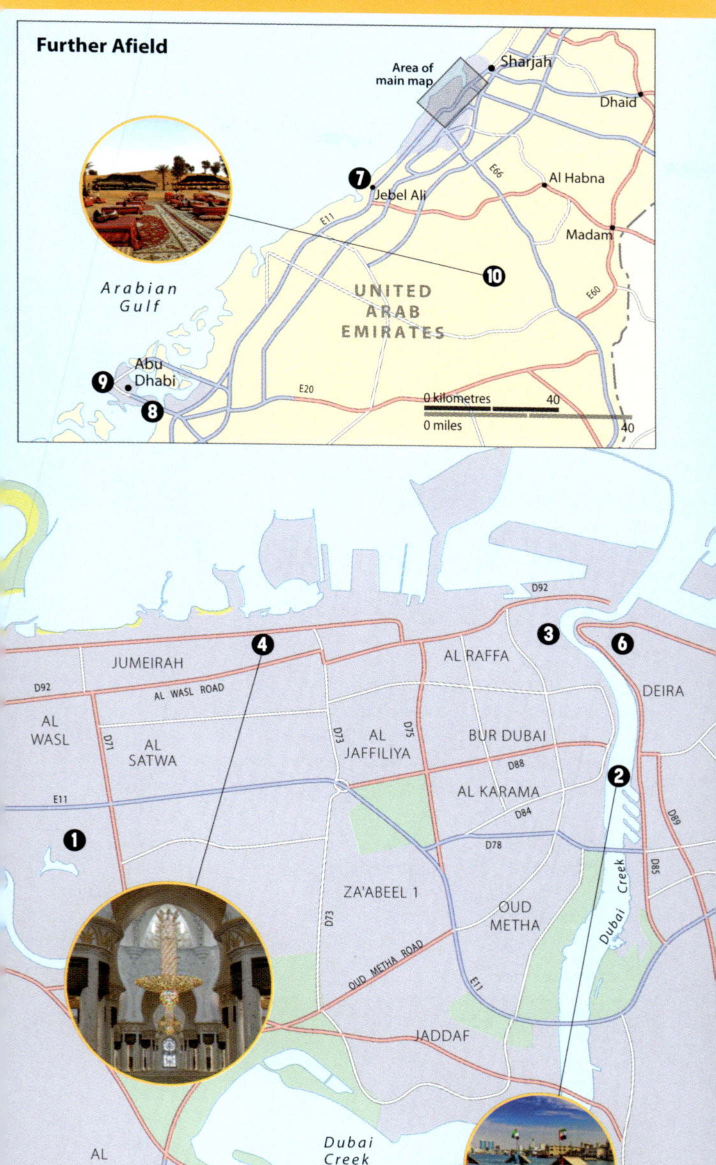
Further Afield
Area of main map
Sharjah
Dhaid
E66
Al Habna
Jebel Ali
E11
Madam
Arabian Gulf
UNITED ARAB EMIRATES
E60
Abu Dhabi
E20
0 kilometres 40
0 miles 40
D92
JUMEIRAH
AL RAFFA
DEIRA
D92
AL WASL ROAD
AL WASL
D71
AL SATWA
D73
AL JAFFILIYA
D75
BUR DUBAI
D88
AL KARAMA
E11
D84
D89
D78
D85
ZA'ABEEL 1
D73
OUD METHA
Dubai Creek
OUD METHA ROAD
E11
JADDAF
Dubai Creek
AL MARQADH

1

BURJ KHALIFA AND AROUND

C6

Opened in 2010, the Burj Khalifa is by far the tallest building on the planet (828 m/2,716 ft). Its needle-thin outline soars high above the city skyline and is visible from almost 100 km (62 miles) away. Surrounding this iconic building are towering skycrapers, luxurious hotels, cultural arts centres and, just beyond, the heritage district of Old Dubai.

1 Exhibition, Burj Khalifa

The Burj's *(p75)* entrance foyer and the route to the observation decks feature interesting displays and chart the history of the building's construction, commemorating some of the leading figures involved. A display of fascinating photos also shows the tower when it was under construction.

Dining area at the Armani Hotel

2 Armani Hotel, Burj Khalifa

armanihotels.com

Spanning several of the Burj Khalifa's lower floors is the flagship branch of the luxurious Armani Hotel. It has trendy bars and restaurants, which are open to non-guests.

3 At.Mosphere Burj Khalifa

The world's highest bar and restaurant *(p79)* is on

Burj Khalifa rising above the city

TOP TIP

Tickets for Burj Khalifa's observation decks are cheaper if pre-booked on the website.

the Burj's 122nd floor. Its theme is fine dining and cocktails in the clouds.

4 Observation Decks, Burj Khalifa

The two observation decks offer incredible views for miles around. The views straight down over Downtown Dubai are particularly stunning, with buildings, appearing almost like neat models, clustered around the intense blue outline of the Burj Khalifa Lake.

5 The Dubai Mall

Tucked beneath the Burj Khalifa, the Dubai Mall *(p77)* is home to varied shops and attractions. Highlights include an aquarium, an ice rink, the immersive KidZania *(p49)* and a real dinosaur fossil, the Dubai Dino.

6 The Address Downtown

Sheikh Mohammed bin Rashid Blvd **the address.com**

Dominating the view to the southeast of the Burj is this huge 72-storey hotel, with an unusual semicircular summit. Head to Neos cocktail bar on the 63rd floor for a different perspective of Downtown Dubai.

7 Dubai Opera

Sheikh Mohammed bin Rashid Blvd **Box office: 11am–8pm daily** **dubaiopera.com**

Nestled next to the Burj Khalifa, this performing arts centre is Dubai's top creative destination, hosting among the finest theatre performances, opera, concerts, ballet and exhibitions from around the globe.

8 Sheikh Zayed Road

North of the Burj, Sheikh Zayed Road features a long line of spiky skyscrapers, mostly housing residential and office complexes. Take a stroll down this busy avenue for an insight into the daily life of Dubai's ultra-rich residents.

9 Outdoor Art

Downtown Dubai is home to a collection of outdoor art installations, notably the *Wings of Mexico* by Mexican artist Jorge Marín and *Love Me* by British sculptor Richard Hudson.

10 Souk Al Bahar and Old Town

On the southern side of the Burj Khalifa Lake is Souk Al Bahar *(p76)*. This area marks a significant change in architectural tone with sand-coloured, Arabian-style design.

VIEW

In the evening, visit the Burj Khalifa's illuminated lake to watch the wonder fully choreographed Dubai Fountain *(p75)* water show.

2

DUBAI CREEK

K1–K4

Fed by the waters of the Arabian Gulf, the Dubai Creek is the lifeblood of both old and new Dubai. The contrast of traditional wooden *dhows* at the wharfage against stunning modern architecture is striking. The two sides of the creek are Deira (north) and Bur Dubai (south). Cross it using the Maktoum and Garhoud bridges or take a traditional *abra*.

1 Dhow Wharfage

Stroll beside the creek along Baniyas Road, where colourfully painted wooden *dhows* *(p65)* are moored and boats arrive from Iran, Oman and the rest of the UAE.

2 Abra Trips

Route 1: 5am–midnight; Route 2: 24 hours

Dubai's open-sided, flat-bottomed water taxis, known as *abras*, offer a breezy way to travel along the creek and provide lovely city views. Route 1 runs between the Deira Old Souk Station and the Bur Dubai Station, while Route 2 connects the Al Sabkha Station and the Dubai Old Souk Station. Buy tickets directly from the *abra* drivers. For private trips, enquire at the stations.

DRINK

Stop for a chilled glass of fresh fruit juice at the bustling Textile Souk *(p70)*, located near the creek's entrance in Bur Dubai.

3 Creek Cruises

dhowcruisetour.com

Scores of tour operators offer romantic dinner cruises along the creek each evening aboard traditional wooden *dhows*, often accompanied by belly dancing and live Arabian music. The sleek Bateaux Dubai *(bateauxdubai.com)* offers a more modern and luxurious option.

Historic Ruler's Court (Diwan)

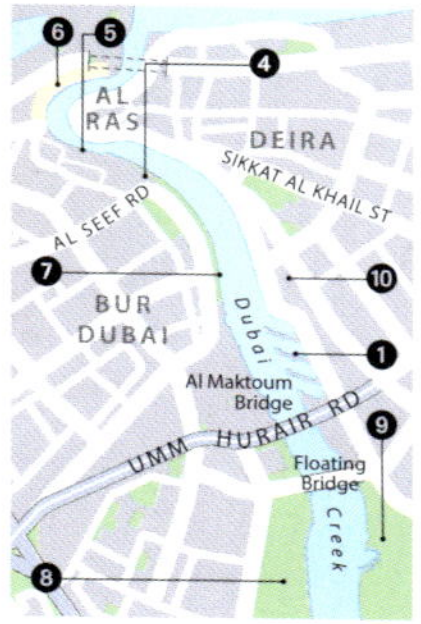

4 Ruler's Court (Diwan)

With its modern white windtowers and imposing wrought-iron gates, the Diwan *(p69)* is an important building housing the offices of the Dubai ruler.

5 Bur Dubai Waterfront

K2

The Diwan and architecture of Old Dubai are best enjoyed from the Deira side of the creek: here you can see windtowers, minarets and the domes of the Grand Mosque.

6 Shindagha Heritage

J1

In the Shindagha area near the mouth of the Dubai Creek, you will find the Al Shindagha Museum *(p70)*, which includes a group of heritage houses and an exhibition charting the development of the city since its birth.

7 Al Seef

K2–K3 10am–10pm daily (to midnight Thu & Fri)

Sprawled along the creek's shoreline, Al Seef was once home to pearl divers, weavers and traders. It now offers a charming blend of culture and heritage, with shops and restaurants tucked along the marina.

THE CREEK AND THE CITY

Dibei, as the city was known in the 16th century, owes its existence to the 14-km (9-mile) creek that then stretched through it. The creek's natural harbour allowed Dibei to transform itself from a tiny fishing village to a flourishing trading hub.

Enjoying an *abra* ride across Dubai Creek

8 Creek Park

E2 8am–11:30pm Thu–Sat, 8am–11pm Sun–Wed dm.gov.ae

Stroll along this expansive waterfront park to enjoy vistas of the creek. You can also enjoy a round of mini golf or go-karting here.

9 Dubai Creek Golf and Yacht Club

This building *(p63)* is one of the city's most unusual Modernist landmarks, with glass-fronted façades nestled beneath three spiky white "sails".

10 Emirates National Bank of Dubai

One of Dubai's very first Modernist high-rises *(p64)*, this is still one of its most memorable. Its curved façade reflects the water below.

AL FAHIDI HISTORICAL NEIGHBOURHOOD

K2

The beautifully restored Al Fahidi quarter (formerly called Bastakiya) offers a glimpse into Dubai's past. In the maze of shady streets and alleys are traditional windtower houses, complete with elegant courtyards, Arabesque windows and decorative gypsum panels. There are also a number of art galleries, museums and cafés.

1 Traditional Architecture

The need to remain cool prompted the vernacular style of the windtower courtyard houses. Thick walls and narrow windows with intricate Arabesque designs are featured.

2 Majlis Gallery

Named after the Arabic word for a meeting place, Majlis *(p44)* is a bijou art gallery built around a beautiful Arabic house and garden. It displays works of both local Emirati and expat artists, including original crafts, pottery, ceramics and jewellery.

3 Coins Museum

800 33222

8–11:30am Fri

The Coins Museum showcases Arabian money through the ages. Almost 500 coins are on display, from Ummayad to Ottoman times, with touchscreens providing historical information.

TOP TIP

Visit Al Fahidi late in the day when the golden light and long shadows add to the setting.

4 Sheikh Mohammed Centre for Cultural Understanding

This pioneering centre *(p69)* provides a deeper understanding of Emirati culture. Many activities are available, including walking tours of Al Fahidi *(p59)* and "cultural" breakfasts and lunches.

Ornate décor, Coffee Museum

EAT

For lunch, the Arabian Tea House Café *(p73)* offers a great Lebanese and Middle Eastern menu of healthy light meals and snacks, fresh soup and salad.

5 Coffee Museum

This museum *(p70)* reveals the history of the region's favourite drink – coffee. Exhibits include old-fashioned grinders, coffee pots and antique tins. Be sure to try the Arabian-style coffee.

6 Old City Wall

Restoration work of the original 200-year-old city wall has drawn attention to the history of this section of the city as a crucial defensive zone.

7 Al Fahidi Fort

This fort *(p69)* is Dubai's oldest building, built in 1787. Its original walls were built from coral and shell rubble.

8 Local House Restaurant

Famous as the first restaurant in the UAE to serve camel burgers, Local House *(p73)* is a friendly neighbourhood restaurant inspired by the local culture and flavours of Emirati cuisine. It offers delicious meals in a traditional setting in the Al Fahidi neighbourhood.

9 XVA Gallery, Café and Hotel

The courtyard of this restored traditional house *(p45)* features galleries that showcase contemporary artworks. It is also home to a café and hotel *(p114)*.

WINDTOWERS

The most distinctive architectural element of Arabian houses in the early 20th century, windtowers *(barjeel)* create natural ventilation. With four open sides, each hollowed into a concave V-shape, windtowers deflect the air down, cooling the rooms below. Water was usually thrown on the floor beneath the tower for further cooling.

10 Arabian Tea House Café

Set in the charming courtyard of one of the houses in the neighbourhood, this café *(p73)* is the perfect spot to relax and enjoy lunch amid the flowering bougainvillea.

Clockwise from right **Collection of rare coins at the Coins Museum; historic Al Fahidi Fort; diners enjoying a meal at the Arabian Tea House Café**

JUMEIRAH MOSQUE

E4 Jumeirah Beach Rd, Jumeirah For tours: 10am, 2pm Sat–Thu
jumeirahmosque.ae

Originally a gift to the people of Dubai, the Jumeirah Mosque has since become a defining cultural landmark and a jewel in the city's crown. It was built in 1979 and is a fine example of modern Islamic architecture, with its smooth white-stone façade, elaborately decorated twin minarets and a majestic dome. Its remarkable features are especially breathtaking when illuminated at night.

1 Exterior

Built in the Fatimid style that originated in Syria and Egypt, this structure features a vast central dome, surrounded by four smaller domes. Two slender minarets, rounded at the top, frame the domes. Keel arches, latticed windows and intricate geometric relief work embellish the façade.

2 Minarets

Two minarets crown this mosque, rising to a height of 70 m (230 ft). The height of the minarets – the highest points of the "House of Allah" – were determined by how far the call to prayer should be heard.

TOP TIP

Dress conservatively; avoid shorts and sleeveless tops. Women must don a headscarf.

3 Ablutions Fountains

Fountains and taps in the outer courtyard are used for the purpose of washing the face, arms, neck and feet. This is considered an integral part of the act of prayer.

4 Prayer Hall

Inside, the walls are painted in shades of pastel blue, peach and beige. They are inscribed with Qur'anic calligraphy in the Arabesque style. There are also elegant arches and columns, wooden doors, stained-glass windows and grand chandeliers.

Twin minarets of the mosque

5 Minbar

The *minbar* is the pulpit from which the *imam* (leader of prayer) stands to deliver the *khutba* (Friday sermon).

6 Mihrab

The *mihrab* is the niche in the wall of this and every mosque. Its purpose is to indicate the *qibla*, the direction one should face when praying. It is meant to give the impression of a door or a passage to Mecca.

7 Once Upon a Time Museum

Learn about the history of Dubai and the UAE at this small museum, which displays artifacts and photographs from the 1970s and 1980s.

8 "Open Doors, Open Minds" Guided Tours

One of the few mosques in Dubai open to the public, the Jumeirah Mosque can be visited only on a guided tour organized by the Sheikh Mohammed Centre for Cultural Understanding *(p69)*. The tour offers a great opportunity to gain insight into the Islamic faith and Emirati culture and includes a Q&A session at the end. Pre-booking is not essential, but note that registration opens at the *majlis* 30 minutes before the tour begins.

CALL TO PRAYER

Wherever you are in Dubai, you are likely to be within earshot of a mosque and hear the daily calls to prayer *"Allahu akbar"* (God is great). In the past, the muezzin made the call himself. Today, it is transmitted through loudspeakers; several speakers are attached to the tall minarets of the mosque for this purpose.

Visitors on a guided tour of the mosque

9 Majlis

The tour of the mosque begins at the vast *majlis*, or the reception hall. There's also a small gift shop here and a dining area where traditional Emirati refreshments are served at the start of the tour. Photography exhibitions on Islam and mosque architecture are also hosted here.

10 Ramadan Celebrations

The mosque is busiest during the holy month of Ramadan (the ninth month of the Islamic calendar). Its façade is beautifully illuminated with dazzling lights during this period.

EAT

A short five-minute drive from the mosque is the multi-award-winning Orfali Bros bistro *(p85)*, which is considered the best restaurant in the UAE.

Once Upon a Time Museum

JUMEIRAH BURJ AL ARAB

C1 Umm Suqeim 3, Dubai jumeirah.com

The iconic sail-shaped Jumeirah Burj Al Arab (meaning "Beautiful Arabian tower") has become an international symbol for modern Dubai. The exclusive all-suite hotel, with its helipad and a restaurant seemingly suspended in mid-air, offers sheer decadence. Set on its own artificial island, it is dazzling white by day and rainbow-coloured by night, with spectacular light displays.

Regal furnishings in one of the suites

1 Exterior

The shore-facing façade of the Jumeirah Burj Al Arab is covered by what looks like stretched translucent fabric. This is Teflon-coated woven glass fibre. It is the first time in the world that such technology has been used this way for any building.

2 Lobby

The lobby of the tower is an airy space of marbles, mosaics and handcrafted carpets in swirling patterns. There is an impressive multi-hued dancing fountain.

3 Fish Tanks

A pair of huge tropical aquariums dominate the lobby. They are so large that the hotel staff don diving suits to clean them.

4 Atrium

The atrium's vast gold-leaf-covered columns, and the many layers of floors rising up from the lobby, create a dizzying sensation for onlookers.

HOTEL GUIDE

To enter for any purpose, you must have a reservation for a meal, cocktails or afternoon tea. Call the hotel at 04 301 7600 to reserve a table. The most affordable options are drinks at Gold On 27 and at Scape Restaurant & Bar, or food at Bab Al Yam restaurant.

5 Suites

The 202 amazing duplex suites are well equipped with the latest remote technology, plus in-suite check-in and personal butler service. The Royal Suite has been converted into a museum offering tours of the luxurious hotel room.

6 L'Olivo at Al Mahara

6:30–10pm daily

At the base of the tower, this lavish seafood

Impressive *dhow* sail of the Burj

Aerial view of the Burj's helipad

restaurant is helmed by chef Andrea Migliaccio of the Michelin-starred Ristorante L'Olivo in Capri.

7 Talise Spa

8am–9pm daily

Perched on the 18th floor, Talise Spa is an idyllic retreat with soothing ocean views. Its beautiful decor is reminiscent of baths used by ancient Middle Eastern civilizations. The infinity pools offer panoramic views.

8 Skyview Bar

With its sky-high location, this rooftop bar *(p52)* offers amazing vistas of the shimmering coastline and guests transferring along the causeway. The bar – a must for cocktails at sunset – is reached by an express panoramic lift.

9 Helipad

Jutting out of the tower's summit, the building's iconic helipad has featured in numerous commercials and is used as a method of arrival or departure by wealthy guests. It has also served as a very unique wedding venue, and once hosted a game of tennis between legendary players Andre Agassi and Roger Federer.

10 Architectural Inspiration

The billowing sail of the Arabian *dhow* was the inspiration for this contemporary creation.

THE TOWER'S CONSTRUCTION

The Jumeirah Burj Al Arab is said to be one of the most expensive buildings ever constructed. An estimated US$2 billion was spent on it, though the full cost has never been revealed. Built on its own artificial island (which took three years to reclaim), the building rises to 321 m (1,053 ft); it was the world's tallest hotel until 2007. Inside, the dazzling décor features more than 30 types of marble and 8,000 sq m (86,111 sq ft) of shimmering 22-carat gold leaf ornamentation.

6

DUBAI SOUKS

J1 10am–10pm daily (some shops shut at 1:30pm for afternoon prayers and have reduced hours on Fridays)

Away from Dubai's glitzy malls is a delightful shopping experience: the souks. Many of these, such as the gold, textile and spice souks clustered beside the creek, date back to the city's beginnings as a trading port. Typically, similar types of stall, selling spices, crafts or clothing, are located close together, making it easy to spot a good deal.

1 Naif Souk

L2 Naif Rd, Deira

A kitsch faux-desert fort houses this traditional-style souk, which sells everything from leather goods to electronics. It's popular with local women for abaya cloaks.

2 Gold Souk

Gleaming with gold, silver and gems, this souk *(p64)* offers great value at competitive prices. Dealers come in from around the globe and strict regulations are followed.

TOP TIP

Bargaining is expected. Start at half the initial price until a deal is made.

3 Spice Souk

This tiny souk *(p64)* is a real sensory delight. Visitors can purchase aromatic frankincense and myrrh (with charcoal burners for them), plus a wide array of flavourful dried fruits and spices such as cloves, cardamom and cinnamon. Iranian saffron is particularly good value.

4 Al Seef Heritage Souk

K2 Al Seef St

A delightful modern souk that pays homage to the markets of old, here you'll find a wide variety of handicrafts and accessories, as well as perfumes and many souvenirs.

Clockwise from below
Shopping at the Gold Souk; scent bottles at the Perfume Souk; entrance to the Al Seef Heritage Souk; spices for sale at the Grand Souk Deira

Stalls selling local handicrafts, Textile Souk

5 Grand Souk Deira

Sprawling behind the Spice Souk, Deira's Al Souk Al Kabeer ("Big Souk") *(p65)* contains hundreds of shoe shops clad in coral-stone. The little Al Arsa Courtyard at the back is very pretty.

6 Meena Bazaar

A visit to this souk *(p72)* may necessitate a trip to a tailor. Wonderful fabrics from all over the world, in every colour and texture imaginable (silks, satins, brocades, linens and more), are laid out before you.

7 Textile Souk

Beautifully restored, this creekside souk *(p70)* is covered by an arched pergola. It makes for an atmospheric walkway lined with little stalls selling reels of coloured cloth. You can also find pretty accessories like buttons and lace to spruce up your outfit.

8 Perfume Souk

Shops here *(p64)* sell exquisite scents like jasmine, oudh, amber and rose, and will also mix individual "signature scents". Traditional Arabian *attars* (perfumes) are for sale alongside well-known Western brands.

9 Waterfront Market

Great piles of colourful fruit and vegetables (including a staggering variety of dates), huge hunks of meat and heaps of ocean-fresh *hammour* and shark are just some of the foodstuffs on offer at this bustling souk *(p63)*.

10 Karama Souk

This souk *(p72)* doesn't resemble a traditional Arabian marketplace. Here, you'll find "replica" items of anything you are looking for (especially watches and handbags). Although fake, the products are of very good quality.

VISIT TO A TAILORS

Dubai is a wonderful place for tailoring, thanks to an incredible array of textiles being widely available. Various tailors' shops can be found around the Textile Souk, but also elsewhere in Satwa and Bur Dubai. Most tailors will be able to make an exact replica from the original item or a photograph, or you can select from a range of patterns catalogued in books.

THE BEACH, JBR

B1 thebeach.ae

Sun, sea and family fun await at The Beach, JBR, a development in the heart of Jumeirah Beach Residences. Here you can bounce your way around a water park, break a sweat at an outdoor gym and relax on golden sands. And after the sun goes down, catch a movie or enjoy a delicious meal at this buzzing, waterfront destination.

1 Sea Breeze

8am–sunset daily

This free-to-access beach is perfect for relaxing. Visitors can hire loungers or a cabana, and order food and drink directly to the seat. There are also lifeguards, public bathrooms and lockers for storing belongings.

2 Bla Bla Dubai

10am–3am daily blabladubai.ae

Bla Bla Dubai is a beach club by day and a dining and social hub by night, with bars to suit every mood, from traditional pubs to a Tiki lounge and fun champagne bar.

3 Ain Dubai

Noon–8.30pm daily (from 11am Sat & Sun) aindubai.com

Cross the picturesque pedestrian bridge from JBR to reach Bluewaters Island *(p87)*, home to the world's tallest observation wheel, Ain Dubai. Take a leisurely spin in one of its pods to admire breathtaking views that stretch to Palm Jumeirah *(p86)* and beyond.

TOP TIP

Buy the Ain Dubai View Plus Family Pass to get several benefits, such as "fast queue".

4 Pop-up Markets

During the cooler months (October to April), The Beach's collection of static boutiques is joined by pop-up market stalls selling artisanal goods, handicrafts and local fashion. Live music and street performers add to the lively atmosphere.

5 Roxy Cinemas

10am–10pm daily (to midnight Sun & Sat) theroxycinemas.com

Roxy cinemas are among Dubai's best cinematic

experiences, with their excellent sound quality and luxurious recliners. During the cooler months, there are premium open-air screenings in the evenings, under the stars.

Dining on the promenade of JBR

6 AquaFun Dubai Water Park

Spanning an impressive 2,700 sq m (29,000 sq ft), this is one of the largest inflatable water parks in the world *(p87)*. Slip, slide and leap your way across the many water-soaked obstacles that make up the fun assault course, all while trying to avoid a fall into the drink.

7 Dine at the Pavilion

🕒 10am–midnight Sun–Thu, 10am–1am Fri & Sat

The Pavilion is one of the best spots in Dubai to enjoy alfresco dining. The six eateries here offer an array of global cuisine, from Slavic to pan-Asian, and are among the few restaurants in the UAE that are licensed to serve alcohol.

8 Jogging Track

A rubberized jogging track stretches the length of the promenade here, providing a comfortable path for morning runs when the area is at its coolest. Water fountains along the route keep runners hydrated.

9 Outdoor Gym Stations

Dotted alongside JBR's jogging track are free-to-use gym stations, with equipment including callisthenics bars, parallel bars and other body-weight equipment.

EAT

If you plan to enjoy brunch at La Mezcaleria *(056 520 2020)* on Saturdays (1–5pm), take advantage of the free-flowing food and drinks packages.

10 Street Art

Along JBR's promenade are a series of stark murals. A stand-out is *Giraffes in the Jungle*, a *trompe-l'œil* by the Planet Streetpainting collective, which creates the illusion of animals breaking through the wall.

Looking out over the beach towards Dubai

SHEIKH ZAYED MOSQUE

V3 Khaleej al Arabi and Sheikh Rashid bin Saeed sts
9am–10pm daily (from 4:30pm Fri) szgmc.gov.ae/en

Standing guard over Abu Dhabi, the Sheikh Zayed Mosque is the largest in the UAE, with capacity for 50,000 worshippers. The brainchild of former president Sheikh Zayed bin Sultan Al Nahyan, its design blends Persian, Mughal and Moorish styles, and features marble and gold details. The mosque draws huge crowds on Eid and New Year's Eve.

1 Exterior

The outline of the mosque, with four great minarets, dominates all paths to the city. Covered in white Sivec marble from Macedonia, it is topped with 82 domes. The 5pm Sunset Tour is a good time of day to see the mosque.

2 Entrance

This grand white entry arcade has gold-topped pillars on either side and long pools of water in front.

3 Prayer Hall

The cavernous main prayer hall is an extravagant showpiece of decoration and design, supported by 96 marble-clad columns inlaid with mother-of-pearl. The hall can seat over 7,000 worshippers.

4 Prayer Hall Carpet

The floor of the main prayer hall is covered in a single carpet, the largest in the world. Made in Iran, the carpet covers over 5,000 sq m (53,819 sq ft), weighs around 35 tonnes and contains nearly 2.26 million knots.

5 Prayer Hall Chandelier

Hanging magnificently in the centre of the prayer hall is the largest of the mosque's seven chandeliers. This is the world's third-biggest chandelier – measuring some 10 m (33 ft) wide and 15 m (49 ft) high. It was made using over a million Swarovski crystals.

Courtyard of the Grand Sheikh Zayed Mosque

SHEIKH ZAYED

Former ruler of Abu Dhabi and "Father of the UAE", Sheikh Zayed bin Sultan Al Nahyan (1918–2004) became leader of Abu Dhabi in 1966, replacing his elder brother following a peaceful deposition. He initiated a programme that launched the emirate's transformation from an Arabian backwater to a global destination. In 1971, he also became the first president of the UAE. Famed for his generosity, Zayed remains a revered figure in the country.

TOP TIP

Visit just before sunset, when the mosque's façade gleams in warm light.

6 Qibla

The prayer hall's *qibla* wall (indicating the direction in which Mecca lies) has a golden alcove set into the wall surrounded by the 99 names of Allah written in traditional Kufic calligraphy.

7 Minbar

Sitting alongside the *qibla* alcove is the small *minbar* or pulpit, from which sermons are delivered during Friday prayers.

8 Courtyard

The vast courtyard within the Mosque has space for thousands of worshippers and is dazzlingly bright during the day. The floral mosaic, picked out in marble on the floor, is said to be the largest in the world.

9 Minarets

Four tall minarets stand at each corner of the courtyard, rising 107 m (351 ft) high. Their design fuses Mamluk, Ottoman and Fatimid styles from Turkey and Egypt, symbolizing the diverse traditions of Islamic architecture around the world.

10 Tomb of Sheikh Zayed

Outside the mosque is the tomb of Abu Dhabi's former ruler, Sheikh Zayed bin Sultan Al Nahyan. His simple tomb is as understated as the rest of the mosque is ornate.

The mosque's main prayer hall

YAS ISLAND

W4 yasisland.com

From high-speed thrills to world-class entertainment, Yas Island packs more into its 25 sq km (10 sq miles) than most places do in a whole city. Whether you're riding roller coasters, cooling off in water parks, shopping designer labels or teeing off with sea views, this action-packed hub in Abu Dhabi delivers memorable experiences for everyone.

1 Ferrari World Abu Dhabi

Yas Island, YS1 hours vary, check website ferrariworld abudhabi.com

This was the first Ferrari-branded theme park in the world. It has over 40 epic car-themed attractions, from gentle rides to the Formula Rossa, the world's fastest roller coaster, with speeds of 240 km/h (150 mph).

2 Yas Waterworld

There are rides and slides for all thrill levels at Yas Waterworld *(p48)*, including the region's largest wave pool and the Bandit Bomber, a suspended water roller coaster. The Emirati-themed park spans 15 hectares (38 acres) with zones for all ages.

3 Warner Bros. World™ Abu Dhabi

All your favourite Warner Bros. characters, from Batman and Superman to Bugs Bunny and Scooby-Doo, are at this park *(p48)*. It's one of the world's largest indoor theme parks with 29 rides and attractions divided into six immersive areas.

4 CLYMB Abu Dhabi

Yas Island, YS1 1–9pm Mon–Thu, noon–10pm Fri–Sun clymbabudhabi.com

Whether you want to fly (sort of) or climb, CLYMB has an experience for you. This indoor adrenaline hub offers skydiving experiences for beginners and professionals, with expert instructors on

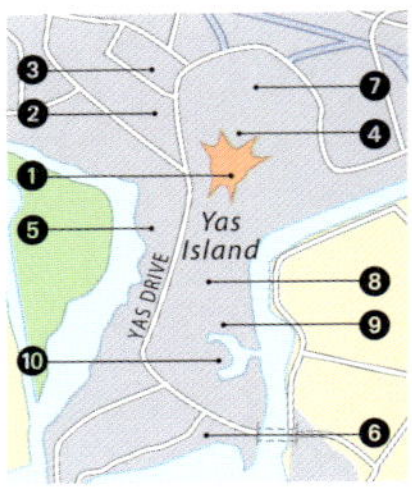

hand, and the region's tallest indoor climbing wall at 43 m (140 ft).

5 Yas Links Abu Dhabi

Yas Island, YS3 6am–9pm daily yaslinks.com

The region's first links course opened in 2010 and is already ranked in the top 100 courses in the world. The facility has an 18-hole championship course, a floodlit 9-hole Par 3 academy course and spectacular coastal views to enjoy while you play.

Yas Marina Circuit

6 Etihad Arena

Yas Drive, YS2 etihadarena.ae

Etihad Arena is the UAE's largest indoor entertainment venue, capable of holding up to 18,000 people. Over the years, the arena has hosted a wide variety of big-ticket

Boats floating in the Yas Marina

events from UFC fights to global music acts such as Coldplay.

7 Yas Mall

10am–10pm daily (to midnight Fri & Sat) yasmall.ae

The largest mall in Abu Dhabi is the place for those in need of retail therapy. It has something for everyone, with over 370 international brands; 68 food and drink outlets, many within a huge fast-food court; Vox Cinemas and KidZania, a role-play centre for children.

8 The Yellow Boats

Yas Marina, Yas Island
9am–8pm daily
yasbay.ae/leisure/the-yellow-boats

Climb aboard a big yellow dinghy shuttle at Yas Marina and set off on a thrilling 75-minute trip around Yas Island. The trip will take you past many of the sights on the island as well as other spots such as Jazeerat Al Sammaliyah Island and the unusual architecture of Aldar HQ *(p100)*, before ending at the lively Yas Bay, home to a collection of highly fashionable bars and top-tier restaurants.

9 Yas Marina Circuit

Yas Central Hours vary, check website
yasmarinacircuit.com

The home of speed in the Emirates is the site of the Formula 1 Etihad Airways Abu Dhabi Grand Prix, which takes place annually towards the end of the year. Outside of the race weekend, the circuit offers year-round driving experiences. Visitors can book a ride or drive a supercar and take a guided track tour.

10 W Abu Dhabi

Built over Yas Marina Circuit, W Abu Dhabi *(p117)* is the only hotel in the world to straddle an F1 racetrack. Known for its distinctive grid-shell design, which lights up at night, it offers incredible track- and marina-view rooms, rooftop pools and several glamorous restaurants.

ABU DHABI GRAND PRIX

First held in 2009, the Abu Dhabi Grand Prix has quickly become a fixture on the F1 calendar and is the only day-to-night race. It is often the season finale and, as such, has seen several champions crowned, including Sebastian Vettel, Lewis Hamilton, Nico Rosberg and Max Verstappen. Most infamously, it was the site of the controversial 2021 finale, where Verstappen overtook Hamilton on the final lap of the season to take that year's title.

DESERT ESCAPES

A trip to Dubai and Abu Dhabi is incomplete without experiencing the myriad textures and colours of the expansive emirates desert. Here, away from the bustle of the cities, camels graze on desert grass and brilliant stars light up the night sky. The terrain is ideal for high-octane 4WD and off-roading tours. Luxurious resorts and Bedouin dining experiences await, too. If you have time, stay overnight and enjoy the peace.

1 Hot-air Ballooning

Drifting over the desert in a hot-air balloon *(p46)* is an incredible experience. A number of reliable operators offer rides over the Dubai Desert Conservation Reserve.

2 Belly Dancing

Belly dancing has a long history in the Middle East. Try to pick up some moves from the dancer at a desert safari – she may even pull you up for a dance.

3 Desert Safaris

Tour agencies such as Arabian Adventures *(arabianadventures.com)* organize desert safaris. Activities may include a thrilling drive in a 4WD, sand skiing, henna painting, sheesha, hearty Arabian buffets and belly dancing performances.

4 Bedouin Feast

Tuck into a delicious Arab buffet, such as the Bedouin feast at Bab Al Shams' Al Hadheerah Desert Restaurant *(babalshams.com)*. You can experience local specialities including *ouzi* (slow-roasted lamb and rice).

5 Spectacular Stargazing

Book a desert astronomy session through tour companies such as Platinum Heritage *(platinum-heritage.com)* to learn about the wonders of the star-filled Arabian sky. They also offer excellent guided nocturnal hikes and informative talks.

An Arabian oryx in the desert of Dubai

6 Desert Camels

Trek through the sand dunes with a local guide, the way Bedouins once did with the stately, majestic camel, a steadfast inhabitant of the desert. Visit the Camel Farm *(thecamelfarm.ae)* to learn how camels are cared for in the desert.

Terrace bar at Bab Al Shams Desert Resort

7 Dubai Desert Conservation Reserve

W ddrc.org

Experience the unspoiled desert at this reserve, with dunes and rare wildlife, including oryx and mountain gazelle. Visit on a day tour or stay at the Al Maha resort.

TOP TIP

Temperatures in the desert are slightly cooler in spring, autumn and winter.

8 Al Maha Resort

Al Ain Road, Dubai W marriott.com

Book a romantic tent-like suite, and get your own plunge pool with the desert as your "backyard".

9 Bab Al Shams Desert Resort

Al Qudra Road, Dubai W babalshams.com

The palm-shaded gardens and trickling ponds make this resort enchanting. A wonderful infinity pool also overlooks the desert.

10 Anantara Qasr al Sarab Resort

This secluded oasis *(anantara.com)* on the outskirts of Abu Dhabi, has traditional hammams, outdoor pools and Arabian food along with arresting desert views.

LIWA OASIS

The most spectacular desert scenery can be enjoyed at Liwa Oasis, which is a few hours to the south of Abu Dhabi by car. The sand dunes here are the largest in the UAE. Beautifully coloured in pretty shades of peach and apricot, the dunes look their best bathed in the sunlight shortly after sunrise or just before sunset.

Cars and a buggy riding the dunes

TOP 10 OF EVERYTHING

A collection of colourful rugs

ART GALLERIES

1 Jameel Arts Centre

E2 Jaddaf Waterfront, Dubai 10am–8pm Wed–Mon (from noon Fri) jameelartscentre.org

Situated on Jaddaf Waterfront near the airport, this beautiful arts space hosts temporary exhibitions celebrating artists from across the UAE.

2 Majlis Gallery

K2 Al Musalla roundabout, Al Fahidi Historical Neighbourhood, Dubai Summer: 10am–2pm Sat–Thu; winter: 10am–6pm Sat–Thu themajlisgallery.com

Dubai's oldest commercial art gallery, Majlis is home to an excellent curated collection of prints, paintings, ceramics and sculptures created by both local and expat artists.

Abstract artwork on display at The Third Line

3 Mavon Gallery

C2 Al Hashemi Building, Showroom 4, Sheikh Zayed Rd, Dubai 050 608 93 07 10am–7pm Mon–Sat

Spanning nearly 929 sq m (10,000 sq ft), Mavon Gallery is Dubai's largest private art space. Designed for discerning collectors, it showcases a superb collection of modern paintings, sculptural works and large-scale installations by renowned international artists.

4 The Third Line

C2 Warehouse 78 and 80, Alserkel Ave, 8th St, Al Quoz 1, Dubai 10am–7pm Sat–Thu thethirdline.com

This gallery displays playful and edgy work by artists from around the Gulf. The exhibits here change every couple of weeks.

5 Efie Gallery

C2 Unit 2, Al Khayat Art Ave, 17th St, Al Quoz 1, Dubai 11am–7pm Tue–Sun efie gallery.com

Using neighbouring Alserkal Avenue as a model, Dubai's Al Khayat Avenue is currently converting warehouses into art spaces. Efie Gallery was among the first to open with an exhibition by African artist El Anatsui, famous for his large-scale bottle-top installations, which have been displayed in New York's MOMA and the British Museum.

Striking interior of the Louvre Abu Dhabi

6 Green Art Gallery

C2 Unit 28, St 8, Alserkel Ave, Al Quoz 1, Dubai 10am–7pm Sat–Thu gagallery.com

Originally opened in Dubai in 1995 as an intimate *salon d'art* dedicated to Arab Modernism, this commercial gallery in Al Quoz displays the work of a multi-generational range of artists from the Middle East, North Africa, South Asia and beyond, with a focus on the heritage, cultures and environment of the Middle East. There is a programme of changing exhibitions throughout the year. These feature a diverse selection of media.

7 Louvre Abu Dhabi

Designed by famous architect Jean Nouvel, the Louvre Abu Dhabi *(p101)* has a unique dome that creates a "rain of light" effect. It is an intricate geometric structure made using 7,850 stars of varying sizes, repeated at different angles. Inside, the museum has diverse artworks from ancient to modern times, including the ancient Egyptian sarcophagus of Princess Henuttawy, which dates back to the 10th century BCE.

8 Manarat Al Saadiyat

A contemporary art gallery, the Manarat Al Saadiyat *(p100)* promotes the creation of art inspired by local culture. It showcases the work of both established and emerging Emirati and international artists. Apart from exhibitions, the gallery also hosts art workshops, poetry nights and music events.

Traditional Arabic façade of the XVA

9 Tabari Artspace

D6 Gate Village, Building 3, Level 2, DIFC, Dubai 9am–6pm Sun–Thu tabariartspace.com

With a mission to nurture local talent, this gallery hosts great exhibitions by Middle Eastern and Emirati artists, laying emphasis on promoting regional female artists. It attempts to bring into focus an understanding of borders, space, place and identity. Highlights here include Mohammed Kanoo's playful Pop Art.

10 XVA Gallery, Café and Hotel

K2 Al Fahidi Historical Neighbourhood, Dubai 10am–6pm daily xvagallery.com

This leading gallery is set in a stylish boutique hotel in a restored traditional house. It offers art consultation services and the idyllic courtyard café also serves as an exhibition space.

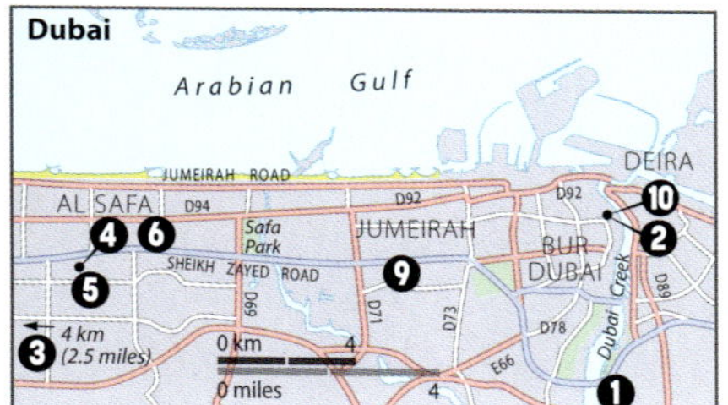

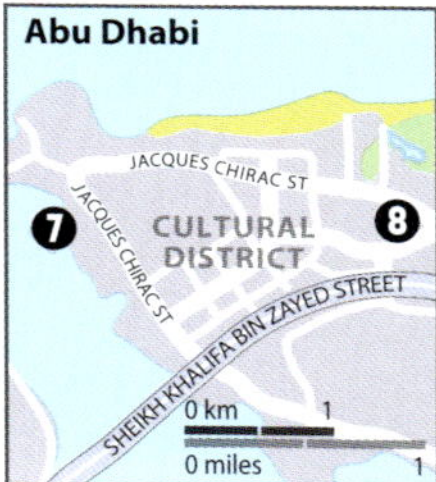

OUTDOOR ACTIVITIES

1 Scuba Diving

The Arabian Sea is home to turtles, angelfish, snappers, barracudas, rays, sharks and dolphins. For the best scuba-diving spots and top diving centres in the UAE, check the Emirates Diving Association website *(emirates diving.com)*. You can also scuba indoors at the aquarium in the Dubai Mall *(p77)* and at the Lost Chambers aquarium at Aquaventure *(p88)*. Wreck diving is also a popular activity along Dubai and Abu Dhabi's coastlines, however many UAE residents prefer diving in Fujairah or neighbouring Oman to explore their rich marine life.

2 Windsurfing

Strong winds make Dubai an ideal windsurfing destination. Most good beach resorts hire out equipment and also offer windsurfing lessons. The Westin Mina Seyahi *(marriott.com)* is particularly renowned for its facilities.

3 Skydiving

For the ultimate Dubai high, strap yourself into a parachute and dive into the city. Skydive Dubai *(skydivedubai.ae)* arranges tandem jumps over the Palm Jumeirah and runs a training school in the desert. Due to high demand, be sure to reserve your spot well in advance.

4 Fishing

Join an organized fishing trip where equipment is provided. Cook your fish on board or charter your own boat. Many resorts *(p114)* in both Dubai and Abu Dhabi offer great fishing trips, check before you book your stay.

5 Karting

Adrenaline-junkies can burn rubber driving pro-karts at the Dubai Autodrome *(dubaiautodrome.ae)*. The 1.2-km (0.7-mile) international standard racing circuit has 17 hair-raising turns. There's also a smaller indoor circuit for children. Book ahead for lessons at the excellent driving school.

6 Hot-air Ballooning

A bird's-eye view of the desert from a hot-air balloon is simply sublime. Only by floating way above the dunes can you fully appreciate the waves of sand and patterns of light and shadow crafted

Skydiving over the Palm Jumeirah

Hot-air ballooning over Dubai's desert landscape

by the ridges that are impossible to see from the ground. Balloon Adventures Dubai *(balloon-adventures.com)* offers rides over the Dubai Desert Conservation Reserve *(p41)*.

7 Wakeboarding

Try your hand at some thrilling wakeboarding tricks on the Arabian Gulf sea. If you're a first-timer, the best place to learn is at a resort. Le Meridien Mina Seyahi Resort & Waterpark in Dubai *(marriott.com)* and the Al Forsan International Sports Resort *(alforsan.com)* in Abu Dhabi offer great lessons.

8 Golf

Both Dubai and Abu Dhabi are awash with world-class courses. Several international competitions take place every year, including the Hero Dubai Desert Classic at the city's largest course, the Emirates Golf Club *(dubaigolf.com)*.

9 Kite Surfing

Kite Beach *(p49)* in Dubai is the place to be for the best kite surfing in the UAE. It has on-site shops where you can hire or buy equipment, as well as instructors to show you the ropes. The best time for kite surfing is from late October to April. Arrive early to enjoy the calmer winds and beat the crowds.

10 Horse-riding

With its world-class Emirates Equestrian Centre *(emiratesequestriancentre.com)*, Dubai is the Middle East's horse-riding capital. There's also a top equestrian club in Abu Dhabi *(adec.ae)*, which offers riding lessons.

TOP 10 SPECTATOR SPORTS

1. Running
The Dubai Marathon *(p57)* and the Dubai Creek Striders Half Marathon *(dubaicreekstriders.com)* are popular among runners.

2. Golf
The world's best golfers compete every year in the Hero Dubai Desert Classic *(p57)* and the DP World Tour Championship *(europeantour.com)*.

3. Tennis
Watch the top tennis players battle it out at the Dubai Duty Free Tennis Championships *(p57)*.

4. Rugby
The national Sevens Stadium in Dubai is home to the Dubai Exiles and the first leg of the Rugby 7s World Tour *(dubairugby7s.com)*.

5. Formula 1 Racing
Since 2009, Abu Dhabi has hosted an annual Grand Prix at the Yas Marina Circuit *(p39)*.

6. Football
Al Nasr (Dubai) and Al Jazira (Abu Dhabi) are the top clubs to watch. The highlight of the season is the UAE Pro League *(uaeproleague.ae)*; catch these matches on weekday nights in winter.

7. Rowing
The Dubai International Marine Club *(dimc.ae)* hosts a year-round calendar of competitive water sports. Prestigious events include the UAE Rowing Championship and the Al Maktoum Cup, which feature traditional wooden rowing boats.

8. Powerboat Racing
Watch lightweight catamarans racing at the F1H2O *(f1h2o.com)* and XCAT *(x-cat.racing)* world championships.

9. Equestrian Sports
Dress to impress for the Dubai World Cup *(p57)*, the world's richest horse race. Other events, like the Dubai Showjumping Championship, are held by the Emirates Equestrian Centre *(emiratesequestriancentre.com)*.

10. Off-road Racing
Bikes, 4WDs and trucks compete in the international cross-country rally of the Abu Dhabi Desert Challenge *(p57)*.

FAMILY ATTRACTIONS

1 Magic Planet

E2 Deira City Centre, Dubai 10am–11pm daily (to midnight Thu & Fri) deiracitycentre.com

An indoor entertainment venue for all the family, with a merry-go-round, bumper cars, video games for children, and a soft-play area for toddlers. There are also branches in Mirdif City Centre *(p54)* and Mall of the Emirates *(p82)*.

2 Ski Dubai Snow Park

All ski levels and ages can try their hand at skiing or snowboarding on the slopes of the largest indoor snow park in the world *(p81)*. There are also a variety of rides here, such as Bobsled, Tubing Run, Snow Bumpers, Zorb Ball and Snow Plough Playground.

3 Dubai Parks and Resorts

B2 Dubai Parks and Resorts HQ, Sheikh Zayed Rd, Dubai 11am–8pm daily (to 10pm Thu–Sat) dubaiparksandresorts.com

The fun never stops at this massive entertainment complex, home to three one-of-a-kind theme parks. At Motiongate, you can enjoy thrilling rides and shows inspired by *The Smurfs*, *Kung Fu Panda* and other popular movies. Real Madrid World attracts fans with ts football-themed rides, while at Legoland®, children can float down a stream on a self-built Lego® raft or earn a "driving licence" in a Lego® car.

4 IMG Worlds of Adventure

C3 Sheikh Mohammed Bin Zayed Rd, Dubai 11am–9pm daily (to 10pm Thu–Sat) imgworlds.com

This indoor amusement park is split into four themed zones, including two based on Marvel Comics and Cartoon Network.

5 Aventura® Parks

Mushrif Park, Dubai 9am–10pm Thu–Sat, 10am–9pm Sun–Wed aventuraparks.com

This adventure park, set in a natural Ghaf tree forest, is scattered with attractions for all levels and ages. Apart from the famous 25-m (82-ft) Tarzan jump, it also features bridges, zip-lines and treetop activities.

6 Yas Waterworld

W4 Yas Island, Abu Dhabi 10am–7pm Sat–Thu, 1–10pm Fri yaswaterworld.com

With fun-filled activities for all ages, this Emirati-themed water park has 45 rides, slides and other attractions.

7 Warner Bros. World™ Abu Dhabi

W4 Yas Island, Abu Dhabi 10am–8pm daily wbworld abudhabi.com

Immerse yourself in the world of Warner Bros. characters and iconic superheroes at this themed park.

Enjoying a water-slide ride at Aquaventure

8 Aquaventure

Spread across 17 ha (43 acres) next to the Atlantis, the Palm *(p116)*, this vast water park *(p88)* has plenty to thrill visitors, along with more gentle river rides that all ages can enjoy.

9 Wild Wadi Water Park

Try some of the 30 adrenaline-fuelled watery rides or just float in a rubber ring along the lazy rivers of this enormous outdoor water park *(p81)*.

10 KidZania

C6 Level 2, Dubai Mall, Dubai Hours vary, check website kidzania.ae

At KidZania, young children take charge in a miniature city where they can role-play different careers, from medics to business tycoons. There's also a branch on Yas Island at Yas Mall *(p93)*.

Role-playing as firefighters in fun-filled KidZania

TOP 10 PARKS, GARDENS AND BEACHES

1. Jumeirah Beach Park
This park *(p82)* has landscaped play areas and a beach with sunbeds.

2. Za'abeel Park
F5–F6 Sheikh Zayed Rd, Dubai 8am–10pm Mon–Thu, 8am–11pm Fri–Sun
A technology-themed park with a football field, boating lake and cafés.

3. Al Seef Road Park
K2 Al Hamriya, Dubai
A lush green space along the banks of Dubai Creek.

4. Creek Park
A botanical park *(p25)* with BBQ areas, a mini-golf course and a cable car.

5. Al Mamzar Beach Park
F1 Al Hamriya, Dubai 8am–10pm daily al-mamzar-beach-park.de
A child-friendly beach park with picnic areas, four swimming beaches, a mini train and bikes for hire. On Mondays, the park is only open to women and girls, and boys under four years.

6. Umm Suqeim Beach
C2 Off Jumeirah Beach Rd, Dubai
Public beach with shallow waters and views of the Jumeirah Burj Al Arab.

7. The Beach at JBR
This is a great spot *(p32)* for water sports or relaxing on the sand.

8. Mushrif Park
F3 Al Khawaneej Rd, Dubai 8am–10:30pm daily (to11:30pm Thu & Fri)
A desert park with pools, farm animals, bicycle tracks, a botanic garden and a theatre.

9. La Mer Beach
D2 2 A St, Dubai
This beach is lined with Jumeirah 1's upscale beach clubs.

10. Kite Beach
C2 Umm Suqeim, behind Wollongong University, Dubai
A popular spot for water sports with plenty of equipment for hire.

LOCAL DISHES

The traditional Arabic vermicelli dish of *balaleet*

1 Balaleet

Balaleet is a sweet-and-savoury Emirati breakfast dish comprised of vermicelli noodles cooked with sugar, saffron and cardamom. These noodles are usually served with a fluffy omelette.

2 Chebab Pancakes with Hatta Honey

Another sweet breakfast staple, *chebab* pancakes are Emirati-style pancakes infused with saffron and cardamom, giving them a fragrant and slightly spiced flavour. They are best enjoyed with a generous drizzle of local Hatta honey and cream cheese.

3 Machboos

Often compared to the South Asian mixed rice dish biryani, *machboos* is a regional rice dish flavoured with *baharat*, a spice mix that's unique to each Emirati family. While its composition varies, it generally features paprika, cardamom pods, cloves and coriander. The spiced rice is then topped with fish, chicken or lamb and black lime *(loomi)* which adds a smoky, tangy flavour.

4 Shawarma

One of the UAE's most beloved street foods, shawarma is a wrap filled with slow-roasted, marinated meat (usually chicken or beef), served with garlic sauce, pickles and fries. Shawarma shops can be found all over Dubai and Abu Dhabi, so you're never too far from your next delicious bite.

5 Slow-cooked Thereed Stew

A true taste of traditional Emirati cuisine, *thereed* is a hearty, slow-cooked stew made with meat, vegetables and aromatic spices. The stew is layered atop *rigag*, a thin and crispy Emirati bread, to scoop up all of the flavours in the broth – it's comfort in a bowl.

6 Um Ali

Referred to as the Emirati version of bread-and-butter pudding, *um Ali* (meaning Ali's Mother) is a comforting dessert made with layers of flaky pastry, nuts, raisins and milk. Legend has it that these ingredients were leftover scraps that the real Ali's mum gathered in a pan and baked, so she could give her son a treat in hard times. It's a common part of the iftar meal during Ramadan.

7 Luqaimat

A favourite at Emirati gatherings, *luqaimat* are small, deep-fried dough balls – akin to mini doughnuts. They should have a crisp exterior and soft, airy interior and be drizzled with date

A bowl of golden *luqaimat* topped with sesame seeds

Breaking apart a delicious *knafeh* dessert

syrup or honey and a sprinkling of sesame seeds for a combination of crunchy and soft textures.

8 Knafeh

Served warm, this dessert – also spelled *kunafa* – comprises layers of crispy shredded filo pastry and molten cheese soaked in rose water syrup and topped with crushed pistachios. Other variants include orange blossom water or nutmeg and cinnamon. Loved across the Arab world, it strikes the perfect balance of crunchy and gooey textures.

9 Dubai Chocolate Bar

There seem to be imposters on confectioners' shelves, but there is only one true version of the famous "Dubai chocolate bar" – and that's FIX Dessert Chocolatiers *(fixdessertchocolate.com)*. The classic flavour is "Can't get Knafeh of it", inspired by the popular Middle East dessert. Its filling is a combination of *knafeh's* shredded filo with pistachio cream. A single bar is AED 68.25, so this may be the most expensive chocolate you'll ever taste, but well worth it.

10 Camel Milk Chocolate

Packed with nutrients and lower in fat than cow's milk, this rich and creamy chocolate is a readily available favourite across the UAE. Home-based brand Al Nassma, located in Souk Al Bahar *(p76)*, claims to have introduced the chocolate to the world, but there are now many chocolatiers throughout the UAE with versions worth trying.

TOP 10 FINE-DINING RESTAURANTS

1. Takahisa
Banyan Tree Dubai **takahisa.ae**
Premium wagyu and sushi are served as part of Japanese *omokase* menus.

2. Ossiano
Crescent Rd, The Palm Jumeirah
atlantis.com/dubai/
The famous "underwater" restaurant at the Atlantis, The Palm *(p116)*.

3. Hōseki
This exclusive nine-seat *omakase* *(p85)* serves sushi made by master chefs before your very eyes.

4. FZN Dubai
Crescent Rd, The Palm Jumeirah
restaurantfzn.com
The first Middle Eastern outpost of Sweden's three-Michelin-star restaurant Frantzén, FZN is world-class.

5. La Petite Maison
Gate Village, No 8
lpmrestaurants.com
French-Mediterranean excellence with a focus on fresh ingredients.

6. L'Amo Bistro del Mare
Dubai Harbour Yacht Club
lamorestaurant.com
Enjoy stunning views of Dubai Harbour while eating at this sophisticated Italian seafood spot.

7. Nobu Dubai
22nd floor, Atlantis, The Palm
atlantis.com/dubai
Nobu serves up a world-famous fusion of Japanese and Peruvian flavours.

8. Sexy Fish Dubai
Level 11, Innovation One
sexyfishdubai.com
Dazzling decor meets high-end Asian seafood and Japanese-inspired dishes.

9. Tasca by José Avillez
Jumeirah Beach Rd
mandarinoriental.com
A vibrant Portuguese dining experience with ocean views.

10. Zuma Dubai/Abu Dhabi
Contemporary Japanese cuisine is served with slick *izakaya*-style service in Dubai *(p79)* and Abu Dhabi *(p97)*.

BARS IN DUBAI

1 Skyview Bar

C1 Jumeirah Burj Al Arab, Jumeirah Rd Noon–2am daily jumeirah.com

Located at the top of the Jumeirah Burj Al Arab *(p30)*, with sweeping views up and down the coast, Skyview Bar is one of Dubai's most atmospheric places for a drink. Advance booking is required.

2 Jetty Lounge

The Jetty Lounge *(p90)* at One&Only Royal Mirage is an elegant beachfront bar with chic Moroccon decor and stunning views of the Arabian Sea. Visit during the cooler months to enjoy well-crafted sundowners in a serene setting.

3 Vault

At the top of the JW Marriott Marquis, Vault *(p78)* is another head-in-the-clouds bar with amazing views across Dubai. Chic decor and cocktails attract a monied crowd.

4 Bar 44

Prop yourself up at the swanky bar or sink into a plush chair at this cocktail bar *(p90)* on level 44 of the Grosvenor House hotel. It draws a regular sophisticated local set as well as visiting businesspeople out to impress colleagues with spectacular views over the bustling Dubai Marina.

Chic interior with stylish seating at Bar 44

5 Mimi Kakushi

D4 Four Seasons Resort, Jumeirah 2 6pm–2am Mon–Thu, noon–midnight Fri–Sun mimikakushi.ae

Featuring in The World's 50 Best Bars in 2024, this exquisite venue transports guests to 1920s Osaka. It is known for its inventive cocktails, notably the

Kiyo-Mizu – a blend of Japanese whisky, Tia Maria coffee liqueur, vanilla and yuzu juice.

6 Asia Asia

B2 Pier 7, Dubai Marina 6pm–2am Mon–Thu, noon–midnight Fri–Sun solutions-leisure.com

This glamorous establishment features a glittering canopy of stars and expertly crafted cocktails. The bar's famed Cosmic Menu offers inventive cocktails inspired by constellations.

7 Nola

With a menu inspired by cuisine from New Orleans, Nola *(p90)* bustles with life every evening. A diverse array of delicious cocktails and Southern American dishes is served here, and the fun vibe is perfectly complemented by the vintage interiors and the weekly live music performances.

8 At.Mosphere

On the 122nd floor of the Burj Khalifa, this is the world's highest bar *(p79)*, offering stunning views in swanky surroundings. Most people come to eat in the attached restaurant, but you can also book for a drink. Advance reservations are required.

9 Bahri Bar

You'll be impressed with the enchanting old-Arabian details and sumptuous interiors of the colonial-styled bar *(p85)* at the Mina Al Salam hotel. Nurse a drink on the veranda and take in the mesmerizing view of the Jumeirah Burj Al Arab.

10 Weslodge

Rock-and-roll meets refined elegance at this chic bar and restaurant *(p78)*. With a selection of classic drinks reinterpreted with an inventive twist, and the best North American cuisine in the city, Weslodge offers a great escape for partygoers and bar hoppers.

Patrons at the Japanese-themed Mimi Kakushi

TOP 10 SHEESHA SPOTS

1. Shimmers
C2 Madinat Jumeirah, Dubai 04 432 3232 Noon–11:30pm daily
Enjoy sheesha at a deluxe beach shack with stunning sea views.

2. Treehouse
D4 Taj Dubai, Business Bay, Dubai 6pm–2am daily (to 3am Fri & Sat) tajhotels.com
Overlooking Business Bay and Dubai Downtown, this rooftop bar is a hidden gem for sheesha lovers.

3. The Courtyard
B1 One&Only Royal Mirage Hotel, Jumeirah, Dubai 04 399 9999 7pm–1am daily
A great selection of aromatic tobacco blends in a cushion-strewn courtyard.

4. Shakespeare and Co
D4 The Village Mall, Dubai 04 344 6228 7am–1am daily
A French Baroque-style patisserie by day, and a sheesha bar at night.

5. Souk Madinat Jumeirah
The central plaza is a breezy, magical spot *(p84)* to smoke sheesha.

6. QD's
Expats love this great smoking spot *(p66)* overlooking the creek.

7. Barouk
W4 Crowne Plaza, Yas Island, Abu Dhabi 02 656 3064 6pm–1am daily
A stylish Lebanese café with a sheesha terrace.

8. Khan Murjan
In the heart of modern Dubai, this restaurant *(p73)* offers sheesha amid the grandeur of a 14th-century souk.

9. Buhayra Lounge
D2 Palace Downtown, Sheikh Mohammed bin Rashid Blvd, Dubai 04 288 8396 8–1am daily
Enjoy a mix of drinks and music along with sheesha at this pool-side lounge.

10. Balcon Lounge & Terrace
T1 Southern Sun Abu Dhabi, Mina Rd, Abu Dhabi 5pm–3am daily southernsun.com/southern-sun-abu-dhabi
An elegant rooftop pool bar offering live music and sheesha.

SHOPPING MALLS AND SOUKS

1 Mirdif City Centre (Dubai)
E3 Sheikh Mohammed Bin Zayed Rd, Dubai 10am–midnight daily citycentremirdif.com
This mall has designer boutiques, many restaurants and entertainment options for both adults and children. It features a thrilling indoor skydiving centre, a sleek IMAX movie theatre and the very popular Magic Planet.

2 The Dubai Mall
Next to the world's biggest tower sits the world's largest shopping mall *(p77)*. This monument to consumerism houses over 1,000 stores, an ice rink, an aquarium, and a vast cinema and entertainment complex. The mall also has more than 150 food outlets, offering everything from fine dining to casual restaurants. For Emiratis, the Dubai Mall is as much about socializing as it is about shopping.

Exploring the luxury boutiques at the Dubai Mall

3 Mall of the Emirates (Dubai)
Over 500 stores, including a chic Harvey Nichols, make this Dubai's most sumptuous mall *(p82)*. If you're in a rush, use the mall's website to identify the best route to the shops you wish to visit.

4 Dubai Festival City
E3 Al Rebat St, Dubai 800 332 10am–midnight Thu–Sat, 10am–10pm Sun–Wed
Located by the waterfront, the Dubai Festival City offers a French Riviera-style marina, excellent shopping and alfresco dining. Its 400 shops include a huge Marks & Spencer and an IKEA.

5 Marina Mall (Abu Dhabi)
This huge mall *(p93)*, in Abu Dhabi, home to over 300 shops and features top luxury brands like Rolex and Tiffany & Co, along with outlets selling traditional Arabian perfumes, sweets and clothing. It also has excellent cafés, including the famous Parisian Hediard.

6 Wafi City (Dubai)
This quirky mall *(p72)* features pharaonic statues, miniature pyramids and hieroglyphics. It is known for its independent fashion boutiques and the Wafi Gourmet deli.

7 Abu Dhabi Mall
Located in the heart of the city, this complex *(p96)* has a wide array

Spacious China Court at the Ibn Battuta Mall

of shops. You can find stores for everything from designer fashion to electronics and home furnishings.

8 Ibn Battuta Mall (Dubai)

A2 Sheikh Zayed Rd, Dubai 10am–10pm daily ibnbattutamall.com

Named after the famous explorer, this themed shopping centre in Dubai has over 275 retailers spread across six courts. The decor for each area is inspired by the countries that Ibn Battuta travelled to: Tunisia, Egypt, Persia, India, Spain and China. There is also a 21-screen cinema.

9 The Galleria (Abu Dhabi)

Set across three floors, the Galleria *(p96)* is one of Abu Dhabi's newest consumer additions. It houses numerous boutique stores owned by world-class luxury brands.

10 Souk Al Bahar (Dubai)

Just over the waterway from the Dubai Mall, this Arabic-themed souk *(p76)* offers a mix of boutique and antique shops. It also has an excellent selection of restaurants and bars, along with spectacular views of the Burj Khalifa – especially when the tower lights up in the evening.

Traditional Emirati textiles on sale at Souk Al Bahar

TOP 10 THINGS TO BUY

Set of *khanjars* (daggers)

1. Arabian Handicrafts
Collectible local handicrafts include traditional Arabian-style coffeepots and *khanjars* (daggers) and miniature carved wooden boxes.

2. Carpets
Buy opulent Persian carpets at prices much lower than you would pay back home. Make sure you bargain hard.

3. Perfume
Concoct your own scent from Arabian oils *(attar)* in a local perfume shop.

4. Gold and Gems
Gold prices in Dubai are among the cheapest in the world. Precious stones (diamonds in particular) are also very keenly priced.

5. Fun Souvenirs
Mosque-shaped alarm clocks, cuddly camels and Burj Khalifa paperweights all make enjoyable mementos.

6. Camel Milk Chocolate
High in natural fats, camel milk makes extra rich and creamy chocolate *(p51)*.

7. Bedouin Jewellery
Chunky antique silver bangles, necklaces and rings make unusual but affordable souvenirs.

8. Music
Stock up on recordings of Middle Eastern music, from traditional Emirati singers to Lebanese pop megastars.

9. Aladdin Slippers
Pick up a pair of traditional curly toed Arabian slippers in the local souks.

10. Electronics
Tight competition keeps prices low for mobiles, laptops and tablets.

DUBAI AND ABU DHABI FOR FREE

1 Jameel Arts Centre

Dubai Creek is the atmospheric backdrop of Jameel Arts Centre's sculpture gardens *(p44)*. Inside, you'll find a roster of contemporary exhibitions that are free to attend, as well as a library dedicated to artists.

2 Sheikh Zayed Mosque

Abu Dhabi's single biggest tourist attraction *(p36)* is absolutely free to enter – and there are even gratis guided tours.

3 Amazing Malls

Some of Dubai's malls are virtual tourist attractions in their own right. Top picks include the extravagantly decorated Ibn Battuta Mall *(p55)* and the upscale Mall of the Emirates *(p82)*, which has surreal views of the snow-clad slopes of Ski Dubai *(p81)*, complete with the occasional penguin.

4 Free Beaches

The huge sandy beach at the Dubai Marina *(p87)* is a popular local destination, with plenty of facilities available, including water sports. In Abu Dhabi, there's a fine stretch of free soft white sand and clear blue sea fringing the city's beautiful Corniche *(p93)*.

5 The Boardwalk

Take a stroll along the boardwalk at Palm Jumeirah. Look out for the remarkable array of luxury resorts along the waterfront, best appreciated at sunset when the hotels become silhouettes on the horizon.

6 Waterside Walks

The breezy walks along the Bur Dubai side (south) of the creek *(p24)* in Dubai and along the Abu Dhabi Corniche *(p93)* are spectacular. You'll see some of the best sights in these intriguing cities and it won't cost you a penny.

7 Ras Al Khor Wildlife Sanctuary

Settle into a hide and watch flocks of bright pink flamingos and other birds, all framed against a surreal backdrop of skyscrapers at this wildlife sanctuary

Strolling along the scenic boardwalk at Palm Jumeirah

(p77). Access to the hides is free, though groups of ten or more will need a permit.

8 Dubai Fountain

Set in the middle of Burj Khalifa Lake, this record-breaking choreographed fountain *(p75)* can be enjoyed for free every evening and most afternoons from any part of the broad pedestrianized walkway running around the lake. This must-see experience offers close-up views of the dancing jets and watery swirls as they rise up, accompanied by dramatic music.

9 Art for Free

Dubai's many art galleries offer endless scope for seeing the work of leading Middle Eastern and other artists at zero cost – unless you want to take a piece home.

10 Free Museums

Museum admission is usually cheap and rarely costs more than a few dirhams, but some places – including the Heritage House *(p63)*, Al Ahmadiya School *(p63)* and the Abu Dhabi Heritage Village *(p94)* – are completely free to visit.

TOP 10 FESTIVALS AND EVENTS

1. Dubai Marathon
Jan W dubaimarathon.org
Runners from around the world take part in this annual marathon race across the city.

2. Taste of Dubai Festival
Feb W tasteofdubaifestival.com
Sample food from some of the city's best restaurants at this mega event in the Dubai Media City Amphitheatre.

3. Dubai Duty Free Tennis Championships
Feb–Mar W dubaidutyfree tennischampionships.com
Top players battle it out at this tennis event held in the Dubai Duty Free Tennis Stadium.

4. Dubai World Cup
Feb–Mar W dubaiworldcup.com
The world's richest horse race, offering a $6 million prize to the winner, is held with great fanfare at the Meydan racetrack.

5. Art Dubai
Mar W artdubai.ae
The Madinat Arena hosts Dubai's biggest contemporary art fair.

6. Hero Dubai Desert Classic
Mar W dubaidesertclassic.com
A renowned golf tournament, the Hero Dubai Desert Classic features the world's top golfers in action.

7. Abu Dhabi Desert Challenge
Apr W abudhabidesert challenge.com
This thrilling four-day motor rally through the desert is unmissable.

8. Sole DXB
Dec W sole.digital
Celebrating footwear, music and art, this annual festival is the highlight of the Dubai Design District's calendar.

9. Dubai Shopping Festival
Dec–Feb W mydsf.ae
A lively, month-long retail and entertainment extravaganza.

10. Global Village
Dec–Feb W globalvillage.ae
A fun-filled multicultural bazaar held in Dubailand on Emirates Road.

EXCURSIONS AND TOURS

Ancient pot at Sharjah's Heritage Museum

1 Sharjah

🏠 10 km (6 miles) N of Dubai

The Heritage Museum *(06 568 0006)*, the Sharjah Art Museum *(06 568 8222)* and the Archaeological Museum *(06 566 5466)* are must-see sights. The souks here are also very good for shopping.

2 Bidiya

🏠 38 km (24 miles) N of Fujairah

This tiny fishing village has the oldest mosque in the UAE, dating back to 1446. Made from mud brick, stone and gypsum, it is now restored, with its four small domes held up by a massive central pillar.

3 Liwa

🏠 300 km (186 miles) S of Abu Dhabi

While Liwa's desert is largely devoid of vegetation, its nearby date farms flourish, creating an eye-catching spectacle. The region hosts the annual Liwa International Festival *(liwainternationalfestival.ae)*, which features cultural events, motorsports and desert camping.

4 Hatta

🏠 105 km (65 miles) E of Dubai

Visit the Heritage Village *(hattaheritage village.com)* at this serene oasis town. A drive into the mountains from here leads to the clear Hatta Rock Pools, a beautiful spot for swimming.

5 Al Ain

🏠 160 km (99 miles) SE of Dubai

Known as the Garden City, this green emirate is home to the popular Al Ain Oasis, a working date farm with 147,000 palm trees. Also located here are the historic Jahili Fort and the Al Ain Camel Souk.

6 Wonder Bus Tour

W wonderbus-dubai.net

This one-hour tour starts with a drive down to Shindagha in Bur Dubai, at which point the vehicle plunges into the creek for a cruise through the old city before returning to land.

7 The Yellow Boats

theyellowboats.com

For the best views of modern Dubai, head out on the water with the Yellow Boats. Tours run up and down the coast starting from Dubai Marina *(p87)*, offering superlative views of the Marina skyscrapers, Atlantis and the Palm, and the Jumeirah Burj Al Arab.

8 Fujairah

130 km (81 miles) E of Dubai

Fujairah offers a refreshing contrast to the UAE's bustling cities, with its rugged landscapes and rich cultural heritage. Stretching along the Gulf of Oman, its coastline is lined with coral reefs and golden beaches, while the dramatic Hajar Mountains rise inland. Its hillsides are dotted with ancient forts and watchtowers, including the impressive Fujairah Fort, the oldest in the UAE, built in 1670. Visitors can explore traditional villages, unwind at luxury beach resorts, or dive and snorkel among vibrant marine life and shipwrecks, making it the perfect getaway.

9 Musandam Peninsula

193 km (120 miles) NE of Dubai

With amazing mountain cliffs and a coastline of inlets and fjords, this northerly enclave is part of Oman. Enjoy *dhow* day trips into the fjords, where you'll often spot dolphins.

Khasab Tours & Travels *(khasabtours.com)* offers tour packages and organizes day trips and excursions.

10 Al Fahidi Walking Tour

Tue & Thu–Sun

Explore Dubai's atmospheric Al Fahidi Historical Neighbourhood *(p26)* with an expert guide from the Centre for Cultural Understanding *(p69)*. The 90-minute morning tours include a rare chance to step inside and explore the neighbouring Ruler's Court *(p69)*.

Rugged mountain terrain of the Musandam Peninsula

AREA BY AREA

Modern skyscrapers in Dubai Marina

DEIRA

Deira is the always buzzing commercial area north of Dubai Creek. It is the source of Dubai's trading roots and it is around the creek that you really get a palpable sense of its origins. There is a telling contrast between the sight of the old wooden *dhows* moored at the wharfside and the glass façades of the sleek skyscrapers that surround them. Much of the cargo carried by these *dhows* is destined for the old souks, including the atmospheric Gold Souk, Spice Souk and Grand Souk Deira, and the newer shopping districts found within Deira. As a result, Deira's winding streets are home to some of the best shopping areas in Dubai. A major preservation effort by Dubai Municipality has ensured that this area has retained some its architectural gems like the Al Ahmadiya School and the Heritage House.

For places to stay in this area, see p114

Manicured greens at the Dubai Creek Golf and Yacht Club

1 Dubai Creek Golf and Yacht Club

E2 Garhoud dubaicreekresort.com

This soaring white building, inspired by the sails of a *dhow* and sitting amid rolling greens, is a city landmark, visible from both the Maktoum and Garhoud bridges. Opened in 1993, this sprawling leisure complex is centred around a world-class golf course. A separate yacht club features a 115-berth marina and two famous restaurants – the Aquarium, known for its excellent seafood, and the Boardwalk *(p67)*, a popular alfresco dining spot, which sits on stilts and offers a spectacular view of the creek, especially at night when the illuminated *dhows* pass by.

2 Heritage House

K1 Al Ahmadiya St 800 33222 8am–7:30pm daily (from 2:30pm Fri)

This beautifully restored airy courtyard house dates back to the 1890s. Its ten rooms are still fitted with ornate 19th-century furnishings. Unusually, this building does not have a windtower; instead the upper floor is designed with open doors and windows to draw in the creek breezes. Now a museum, the building features dioramas and interactive touchscreens that provide deeper insight into the displayed artifacts and the history of the Emirati.

3 Al Ahmadiya School

K1 Al Ahmadiya St 8am–7:30pm daily (from 2:30pm Fri)

Dubai's first school, the Al Ahmadiya School was founded in 1912 by a philanthropist pearl merchant. Subjects such as mathematics, the Qur'an and Arabic calligraphy were taught, and the pupils (all male) sat on palm mats. Many such schools were located in Emirati coastal cities with the support of leading merchants and sheikhs, who subsidised the education. This school closed in 1963 and is today a museum, which offers a great educational insight into the past. It is worth visiting just for its sheer architectural grace.

4 Waterfront Market

L1 Al Khaleej Rd waterfrontmarket.ae

The sights and smells of a traditional food market offer an enthralling insight into the shopping and eating habits of locals in Dubai. On the north side of Deira, this large warehouse-like complex is the old city's major source of fresh food. The colourful fruit and vegetable selection has dozens of stalls piled high with produce, as well as a section specializing in dates. The meat section is for dedicated carnivores only, while the fish and seafood section has over 350 seasonal varieties of seafood, including ocean-fresh prawns, *hammour* and sharks.

Dazzling array of jewellery at the Gold Souk

5 Gold Souk

K1 Al Khor St

You are unlikely to have ever seen so much gleaming gold as in Dubai's historic Gold Souk, with shops selling fine jewellery in both Arabic and Western styles. The souk is still dominated by Indian and Iranian artisans and traders, as it has been for nearly a century. It has been restored with a traditional Arabic arcade and an arching wooden roof.

6 Perfume Souk

K1 Sikkat Al Khail Rd

Just east of the Gold Souk is an array of stores selling a mix of international brands and local perfumes – unlike a traditional souk, the shops here line the street, creating an open-air market vibe. The best are made using the aromatic oud (derived from aloe wood) and come in ornate cut-glass bottles. Most shops also allow you to create your own scents from their selection of perfume oils.

7 Emirates National Bank of Dubai

K3 Baniyas Rd

Another architectural achievement is the building housing the Emirates National Bank of Dubai – one of the city's first iconic buildings. Built in the mid-1990s by Carlos Ott, architect of the Opéra de la Bastille in Paris, it is inspired by the *dhow*. Its curved glass curtain wall symbolizes the billowing sail. Its base is clad in green glass, representing water, and its roof is cast in aluminium (denoting the hull of the boat). It is most striking at sunset, when the glass reflects its gold and silver lights.

8 Spice Souk

K1 26 34 St, off Al Abra St

Moody and atmospheric, the Spice Souk is a sensory trip into the past, where you can wander through a maze of narrow alleyways of shops piled

high with aromatic spices. Take an *abra* (water taxi) to the souk, where you'll find sacks of cinnamon sticks, cumin, coriander seed and oud. Some great souvenir buys include frankincense, henna kits (for hand and body decoration), saffron and fragrant rose water.

9 Grand Souk Deira

K1 34 23C St, off Al Abra St

A fascinating area to wander around, this is where you get a real taste of the melting pot of cultures that is Dubai. Frequented by both Emiratis and expats, this souk offers a wide variety of items, including bright Indian clothing, perfumes, herbs and spices, colourful shawls and fabrics.

10 Dhow Wharfage

K4 Baniyas Rd

A walk along the wharfside beside Baniyas Road allows you to get up close to the painted wooden *dhows*, the traditional Arabian sailing vessels moored here. These ships still trade around the Gulf. Their cargo these days is tyres, refrigerators, air conditioners, electronics – just about any modern item. Moored five or six abreast, these *dhows* have sailed to trade with Dubai from places such as Pakistan and Sudan since the 1830s.

DEIRA HISTORY

Liberal trade policies have backed the development of Deira, which had become the largest souk on the Arabian coast by the early 20th century. It was a haven for merchants who left Lingah, on the Persian coast, after high customs were introduced there in 1902. They continued to trade with Lingah, as do many of the *dhows* in the creek.

Wide range of spices and herbs for sale, Spice Souk

A STROLL THROUGH THE SOUKS

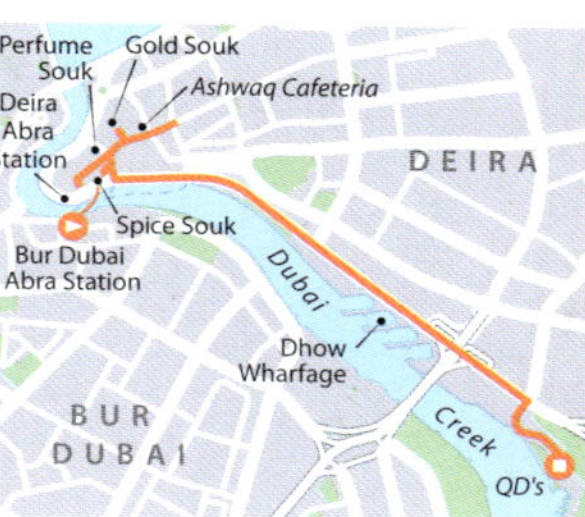

Afternoon

Begin this walk around 4:30pm, when souk shops re-open after prayers and temperatures are cooler. Start with an *abra* crossing from the **Bur Dubai Abra Station** and disembark at Deira Old Souk Abra Station. Take the underpass below Baniyas Road to emerge at the **Spice Souk** entrance and browse the fragrant alleyways. Leave the Spice Souk at Al Abra Street, turn right along Al Ras Street into Sikkat Al Khail Street. Ahead you will see the latticed entrance to the **Gold Souk**. There are more than 300 jewellery shops here (most accept credit cards).

Wander into the narrow alleyways and enjoy a traditional cup of tea at one of the small cafés.

Exit the Gold Souk and continue along Sikkat Al Khail Street to the **Perfume Souk**. Its shop windows are filled with countless bottles of rich Arabian scents, incense and oud.

Evening

Continue along Sikkat Al Khail Street for an evening snack at **Ashwaq Cafeteria** *(04 226 1164)*, a down-to-earth café serving shawarmas. Next, return to the creek to admire the **Dhow Wharfage**. For a relaxed ending to the day, drop in at Dubai Creek and Yacht Club's **QD's** *(p66)* and chill out with a cocktail.

Cafés and Bars

Terrace bar overlooking the creek at QD's

1. YUM!

L2 Radisson Blu Hotel Noon–11pm daily radissonhotels.com/en-us/hotels/radisson-blu-dubai-deira-creek

"Live Fast: Eat Fast" is the motto of this noodle kitchen. Inspired by different Asian cuisines, it makes for a fun pit stop for lunch or a quick dinner.

2. Aroos Damascus

L3 Al Muraqqabat Rd 04 221 3673 7am–3am daily

One of the city's best cheap Middle Eastern cafés, with a menu of mezze, grills and fish, all beautifully cooked. Try to get a table on the terrace.

3. Vivaldi

K3 Sheraton Dubai Creek Noon–midnight daily vivaldidubai.com

This Italian restaurant is ideal for an aperitivo or a post-dinner cocktail.

4. PappaRoti

E2 Deira City Centre 9am–11pm daily (to midnight Fri & Sat) papparoti.ae

PappaRoti is great for a quick bite while taking a break from exploring the city. Try golden-crusted buttered buns, and delicious beverages including teas, flavoured coffees and juices here.

5. Pierre's TT

K3 Promenade Level, Dubai Festival City 4pm–2am Mon–Sat pierresdubai.com

Helmed by famed chef Pierre Gagnaire, this waterfront gem offers refined French cuisine and expert mixology.

6. Paul

E2 Deira City Centre 04 295 8404 9am–11pm daily

This bustling French brasserie chain has taken the city by storm with its excellent sandwiches, salads and eggs Benedict.

7. Cielo Sky Lounge

E2 Dubai Creek Resort Hours vary, check website dubaicreekresort.com

Cielo is the perfect spot for a sundowner or a fun night of music and dance. Its terrace bar offers great views of the Dubai skyline.

8. Irish Village

E2 Garhoud 11am–1am daily (to 2am Thu & Fri) theirishvillage.com

Throw back a pint and tuck into some fish and chips in Guinness batter at this Irish-style pub. The outdoor bench seating is an added delight.

9. Belgian Beer Café

E3 Crown Plaza, Dubai Festival City 12:30pm–2am daily dubaifestivalcityhotels.com

Popular among expats, the BBC, as it is fondly called, offers a variety of Belgian speciality ales and traditional dishes.

10. QD's

E2 Dubai Creek Resort 5pm–2am daily (to 3am Sat & Sun) dubaicreekresort.com/qds-bar-grill

Lounge with a sundowner at this creekside wooden-decked terrace bar or enjoy a sheesha at the *majlis* area while the live band plays.

Places to Eat

1. China Club

L2 Radisson Blu Hotel 04 222 7171 Hours vary, call ahead • DD

This elegant restaurant has striking Chinese decor and an extensive menu of dim sum and Chinese classics.

2. Twiggy By La Cantine

E2 Park Hyatt Hotel, Dubai Creek Resort 9am–2am daily twiggy.ae • DDD

Set on an artificial lagoon overlooking Dubai Creek, this restaurant specializes in Mediterranean cuisine.

3. Thai Kitchen

E2 Park Hyatt Hotel, Dubai Creek Resort 7pm–midnight Sat–Thu, 12:30–4pm & 7pm–midnight Fri hyattrestaurants.com • DD

Thai delicacies are served from live cooking areas. The tasting portions allow you to sample a range of dishes.

4. Seafood Market

E2 Le Meridien Dubai Hotel and Conference Center, Airport Rd 12:30–5pm & 7–11:30pm daily seafoodmarket-dubai.com • DD

This seafood restaurant is revered for its fresh fish presented on ice.

5. Boardwalk

E2 Dubai Creek Resort Noon–midnight daily dubaicreekresort.com • DD

Built on a wooden veranda with views of the creek, this place has a varied menu featuring light Mediterranean fare and Eastern-inspired dishes.

6. Cheesecake Factory

E3 Dubai Festival City Mall 04 419 0874 10am–midnight Thu–Sat, 10am–11pm Sun–Wed • DD

A truly hearty, indulgent restaurant offering a selection of delicious dishes served in wholesome portions, alongside a signature range of mouthwatering cheesecakes.

PRICE CATEGORIES

For a three-course meal for one with half a bottle of wine (or equivalent meal), taxes and extra charges.

D under AED 100 **DD** AED 100–400
DDD over AED 400

7. Fujiya

E2 Millennium Airport Hotel Noon–1am daily fujiya.ae • DD

This is where Dubai's leading Japanese chefs eat on their days off work. Come here for a real taste of Japan.

8. Traiteur

E2 Park Hyatt Hotel, Dubai Creek Resort Hours vary, check website hyattrestaurants.com • DDD

Enjoy classic European cuisine and admire the chic, modern decor here.

9. Anise

E3 InterContinental, Dubai Festival City 6:30–11:30pm daily dubaifestivalcityhotels.com • DD

Enjoy international fare after some shopping at Dubai Festival City Mall.

10. Nomad

E2 Jumeirah Creekside Hotel, Garhoud 6am–midnight daily jumeirah.com • DD

This one-of-a-kind restaurant offers a unique experience with international cuisine and a vibrant decor.

Dining area with exquisite décor at the China Club

BUR DUBAI

This bustling part of the city is packed with hotels, office blocks and residential developments, yet a century ago it was a sandy area filled with *barasti* (palm-frond houses) and windtower houses around the creek. To get a sense of old Bur Dubai visit the historical Al Fahidi neighbourhood (formerly Al Bastakiya), where the charming courtyard houses have been restored, and historic sights such as the Al Fahidi Fort, now the Dubai Museum, are located. It was in this area at the creek mouth, and in the nearby Shindagha heritage area, that Dubai's role as a major trading city began. While some commerce continues to arrive here, this atmospheric district is now a quiet oasis amid Dubai's hustle and bustle.

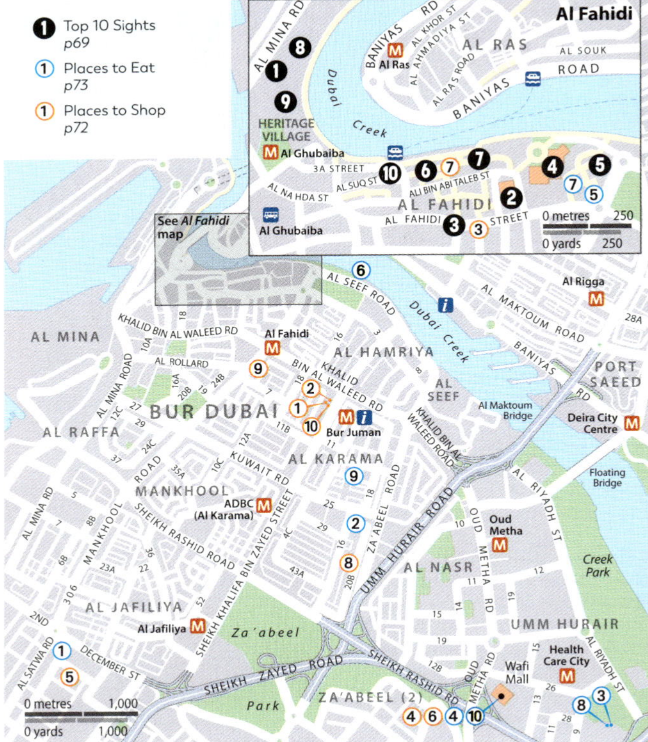

For places to stay in this area, see p114

Traditional buildings in the Al Fahidi Historical Neighbourhood

1 Crossroads of Civilization Museum

J1 Al Khaleej Rd 9am–6pm daily themuseum.ae

Travel through past ages at this intimate museum. The interesting displays here showcase a world-class array of largely Middle Eastern artifacts, which range from ancient Mesopotamia all the way through to the Ottoman era. Highlights include Egyptian mummy masks, priceless Sumerian sculptures and a beautiful section of *kiswa* (cloth used to drape the Kaaba in the Grand Mosque at Mecca), donated by legendary Ottoman ruler Suleiman the Magnificent in 1543.

2 Al Fahidi Fort

K2 Al Fahidi Street, Bur Dubai Closed for renovation

Built in 1787, this fort is Dubai's oldest surviving building. It was originally built to protect the city from invasions, but has also functioned as a royal residence, weapons arsenal and prison. Strategically located near Dubai Creek, the fort played a key role in supporting the city's trade. In 1971, it became the home of Dubai Museum, showcasing local history and the evolution from a pearl-diving hub to a global metropolis. Though it is currently closed, it remains a symbol of Dubai's rich heritage.

3 Al Fahidi Historical Neighbourhood

This is one of the oldest and most atmospheric heritage areas in Dubai *(p26)*. Here you can wander around the alleyways between original, restored courtyard houses. Many are crowned with tall windtowers. Late afternoon is the best time to explore the area, as the light throws the architecture into golden relief. The area has become a cultural hub, with many buildings converted to galleries and courtyard cafés.

4 Ruler's Court (Diwan)

K2 Adjacent to Al Fahidi Historical Neighbourhood, Creekside

A cream building with imposing windtowers sits beside the creek next to the Grand Mosque. The striking gold-topped wrought-iron gates give a clue to its importance: it is the seat of power and the Ruler's Court or *Diwan* (Persian for couch). Dubai's ruler Sheikh Mohammed bin Rashid Al Maktoum's offices are here. You can take a walking tour to explore its interior *(p59)*.

5 Sheikh Mohammed Centre for Cultural Understanding (SMCCU)

K2 Al Fahidi Historical Neighbourhood 8am–4pm daily cultures.ae

The SMCCU was founded in 1998 with the motto "Open Doors, Open Minds". It aims to promote cross-cultural dialogue by providing insight into Dubai's Islamic traditions. Visitors can enjoy immersive heritage experiences, including Emirati meals, mosque visits, city tours and Arabic language classes. The Heritage Express trolley tour of Old Dubai is not to be missed.

Colourful carpets for sale at the Textile Souk

6 Textile Souk

J1 57 Ali Bin Abi Taleeb St

At the heart of Bur Dubai, the Textile Souk begins right by the water's edge at the Dubai Old Souk Abra Station. Following its renovation, the souk is now housed under an imposing arcaded wooden roof, which keeps it cool even during the most consuming heat. It's a mix of old and new – here you'll find moneychangers, textiles, bargain clothes, Arabian slippers and curios. The souk (sometimes referred to as the "Old Souk") is great fun for visitors to explore – look out for the tailors working on old-fashioned sewing machines. Lanes off the main drag are dotted with examples of local traditional architecture, including long wooden balconies, latticed windows and the occasional windtower.

7 Hindi Lane

K1

Buried away at the back of the Textile Souk, this delightful "Hindi Lane" (as it is known locally) is one of Dubai's best-hidden secrets. Walking into this narrow lane is like stepping into India itself, with its colourful shops selling religious posters, garlands of flowers and bindis, and other subcontinental paraphernalia. There is even a tiny Sikh temple right above the shops.

8 Coffee Museum

K2 Al Fahidi Historical Neighbourhood 9am–5pm Sat–Thu coffeemuseum.ae

This fascinating museum dedicated to Arabia's favourite drink spans two floors filled with coffee-related artifacts and accessories. Upstairs there's a coffee bar offering a wide range of superior brews, while downstairs is a gift shop, serving coffee ice-pops, the perfect pick-me-up on a hot summer's day.

9 Al Shindagha Museum

K1 Al Fahidi Historical Neighbourhood 10am–8pm daily alshindagha.dubaiculture.gov.ae

Set along the historic waters of Dubai Creek, Al Shindagha Museum tells the proud story of the nation's past. Highlights of the museum include Perfume House, dedicated to the regional traditions surrounding oud

Door framed by intricate tilework, Iranian Mosque

and the intriguing role of fragrance in Arabian society. Now extended, the original building at the core of the complex dates back to 1896 when it was used as the seat of the ruler of Dubai.

10 Iranian Mosque

J1

Tucked away in a backstreet off the Textile Souk, this superb Iranian Mosque (no entrance to non-Muslims) is tricky to find but well worth the effort. Following the traditional Persian style, every inch of the building's façade and dome is covered in rich *girih*-style tilework glazed with swathes of deep-blue patterns and embellished with delicate arabesques and swirling floral motifs picked out in yellow and green.

MAKTOUM FAMILY'S SETTLEMENT ON DUBAI CREEK

The Maktoum family's reign as rulers of Dubai began in 1833, when Sheikh Maktoum bin Buti and around 800 tribe members broke away from the Bani Yas tribe of Abu Dhabi. They settled in Shindagha, an ideal location for trade and for the development of Dubai's pearling and fishing industries.

Sleek interior of the Al Shindagha Museum

A DAY'S EXPLORATION OF OLD DUBAI

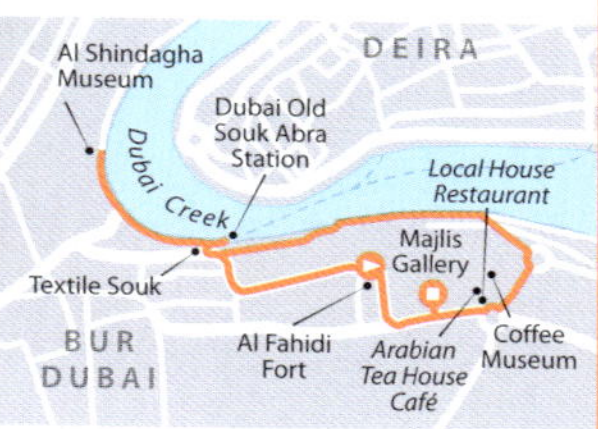

Morning

Start your tour at **Al Fahidi Fort** *(p69)* to experience this remarkable heritage area. Enjoy a glass of fresh lemon juice at any of the nearby waterside restaurants, or visit the coffee bar at the **Coffee Museum** for a taste of Arabia's favourite hot drink – or even a coffee-flavoured ice-pop.

Afterwards, head north up Dubai Creek to **Al Shindagha Museum** to learn about the development of the creek and the history of Arabian perfumes. Following the curve of the creek back towards Al Fahidi Fort, you will arrive at the wooden-arcaded **Textile Souk**. Browse its textile stalls and hole-in-the-wall restaurants. Also peep down the alleyways for views of restored *barasti* wind towers. By the water, you'll see the **Dubai Old Souk Abra Station**. Hop on board for AED 1 rides across the water or take a boat tour. The boat rides offer stunning views of the city's skyline.

Afternoon

Head along Al Fahidi Street to the Al Fahidi Historical Neighbourhood where you can enjoy a leisurely courtyard lunch at the **Arabian Tea House Café** *(p73)*. Afterwards, spend some time exploring the neighbourhood's alleys; don't miss the bijou **Majlis Gallery** *(p44)* and Middle Eastern fare at **Local House Restaurant** *(p73)*.

Luxury boutiques at the BurJuman Mall

Places to Shop

1. BurJuman Mall

J3 Trade Centre Rd 10am–11pm daily burjuman.com

This chic shopping mall features high-end stores selling exclusive labels and glam accessories.

2. Jashanmal "Around the World"

J3 BurJuman Mall 10am–10pm daily (to 11pm Thu & Fri) jashanmal.com

Offering accessories, suitcases and bags from multiple brands, this is the best store for travel essentials.

3. Meena Bazaar

J2 Near Al Fahidi St, Bur Dubai 9am–10pm daily

A network of streets in Bur Dubai, crammed with shops selling a host of intriguing articles such as handcrafted textiles and jewellery, and traditional handicrafts. There are also several Indian restaurants and cafés here.

4. Wafi Gourmet

E2 Wafi City 10am–10pm daily (to midnight Thu & Fri) wafigourmet.com

Stocked with Arabian cheeses and sweets, barrels of olives and dates, plus boxes of Lebanese delights, this is Dubai's favourite delicatessen.

5. Satwa

E5

This suburb is known for its fabrics, tailors and Indian sweet shops. It is where the local people go to shop.

6. Wafi City

E2 Oud Metha Rd 10am–10pm daily (to midnight Thu & Fri) wafi.com

This kitsch, Egyptian-themed, pyramid-shaped building is the best place to head if you love fashion.

7. Textile Souk

Wander through this old renovated souk *(p70)* with small shops and stalls selling a medley of goods, from textiles and shoes to bargain clothing and curios.

8. Karama Souk

H4 Al Karama

Hunt for cheap Arabian souvenirs, handicrafts and designer-inspired goods at this shopping complex. For a sense of local life, wander around the neighbourhood afterwards.

9. Computer Plaza

J2 Al Ain Centre 10am–10pm daily computerplaza-me.com

This shopping centre, with over 60 specialized retail outlets, is the perfect place to pick up a discounted laptop or digital camera. A range of software is also available.

10. Ajmal

J3 BurJuman Mall 10am–10pm daily (to 11pm Thu & Fri) en-ae.ajmal.com

Specializing in Arabic perfumes, which are stronger and spicier than Western fragrances, this store will mix you a signature scent.

Places to Eat

PRICE CATEGORIES

For a three-course meal for one with half a bottle of wine (or equivalent meal), taxes and extra charges.

D under AED 100 **DD** AED 100–400
DDD over AED 400

1. Ravi

E5 Satwa Roundabout
04 331 5353 5am–3am daily • D

Known for its excellent Pakistani cuisine, Ravi offers delicious butter chicken. Note, alcohol is not served here.

2. Calicut Paragon

J4 Opposite Lulu Centre, Al Karama 7am–12:30am daily
calicutparagon.com • D

Savour the coastal cuisine of Kerala, featuring exceptional seafood curries prepared with aromatic spices.

3. Andiamo!

E2 Grand Hyatt Dubai 12:30–3:30pm & 6:30–11:30pm daily
hyattrestaurants.com • DD

This casual Italian restaurant has a cosy outdoor terrace with a floral pergola.

4. Khan Murjan

E2 Souk Khan Murjan, Wafi
10am–midnight daily (to 1am Fri & Sat) khanmurjan.com • DD

A charming courtyard restaurant, Khan Murjan serves Lebanese, Egyptian, Moroccan and Iranian classics alongside traditional Gulf dishes.

5. Local House Restaurant

K2 Al Fahidi Historical Neighbourhood 8am–11pm daily localhousedxb.com • DD

Famous for its camel-meat burgers, this popular neighbourhood spot serves traditional Emirati dishes.

6. Al Fanar

K2 Al Seef 10:30am–11pm daily alfanarrestaurant.com • DD

Atmospheric Al Fanar features recipes passed down by the founder's grandmother.

7. Arabian Tea House Café

K2 Al Fahidi Historical Neighbourhood 8am–11pm daily arabianteahouse.com • DD

For a sense of Arabia, enjoy lunch at this alcohol-free, bougainvillea-clad café in a historic courtyard.

8. Peppercrab

E2 Grand Hyatt Dubai
7–11:30pm daily (to midnight Fri & Sat) hyattrestaurants.com • DDD

Devour a tasty, peppery crab at this Singaporean seafood restaurant (aprons and pliers are provided).

9. Eric's

J3 10 B St, Sheikh Hamdan Colony, Al Karama Hours vary, check website erics dubai.com • D

The wide range of traditional dishes offered at this delightful restaurant have wholesome Goan flavours.

10. Asha's

E2 Pyramids, Wafi City
12:30–3pm & 7:30pm–midnight daily ashas restaurants.com • DDD

Owned by celebrated Bollywood singer Asha Bhosle, this place is known for Indian classics and daring creations.

Interior with a portrait of the eponymous singer at Asha's

DOWNTOWN DUBAI

With a dramatic skyline of futuristic towers, Downtown Dubai has been dubbed "the centre of now" and is home to many of Dubai's iconic landmarks. A drive down the area's main artery, the Sheikh Zayed Road, will take you to the most significant, the magnificent Burj Khalifa, the tallest building on the planet, and the sprawling Dubai Mall, which draws shoppers worldwide, with everything from high street shops to a haunted house and an indoor waterfall. Beyond these architectural giants, the district has also become famous for its chic cafés, luxury hotels and a striking group of public sculptures, all of which can be found on a stroll along Sheikh Mohammed bin Rashid Boulevard. Stick around after dark, when the waters of the Dubai Fountain dance to music in a dazzling spectacle. This is Dubai at its most extravagant.

1 Emirates Towers

D6 Sheikh Zayed Rd
04 330 0000

Two triangular twin towers, the Jumeirah Emirates Towers clad in aluminium and silver glass, soar into Sheikh Zayed Road's skyline. The taller one serves as an office block, where Dubai ruler Sheikh Mohammed bin Rashid Al Maktoum has his office, while the other is home to a 400-bedroom luxury hotel joined by a central podium containing a shopping boulevard. The hotel and boulevard have a great choice of restaurants and bars. Shopping options include fashion from top designers, jewellery and antiques.

2 Dubai Fountain

C6

Filling the space between the Burj Khalifa, Dubai Mall and Souk Al Bahar is the spectacular Dubai Fountain, the world's largest. It features an extraordi-

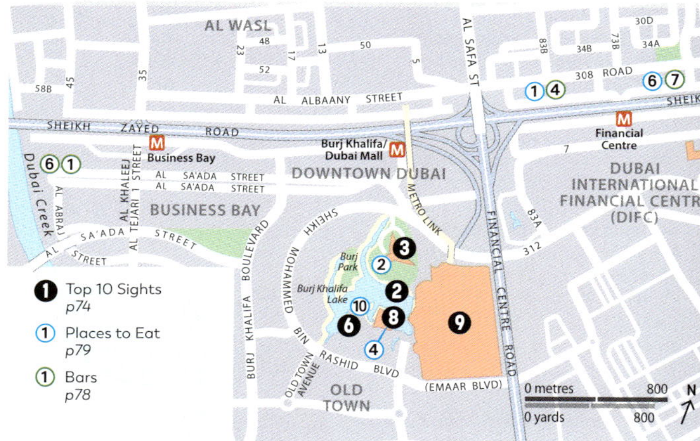

For places to stay in this area, see p114

Spectacular light and fountain show, Dubai Fountain

nary array of jets illuminated with 6,000 lights, which fire plumes of water 150 m (492 ft) into the air. Set in the middle of Burj Lake, the fountain puts on amazing shows after dusk. Every 30 minutes from 6pm to 11pm daily, colourful sprays of water erupt, dancing in sync to an accompanying musical soundtrack. Afternoon shows are also put on at 1pm and 1:30pm, except on Fridays. For a fee, you can get an even closer look at the fountain from a floating boardwalk, or by taking a ride in a traditional *abra* boat across the lake.

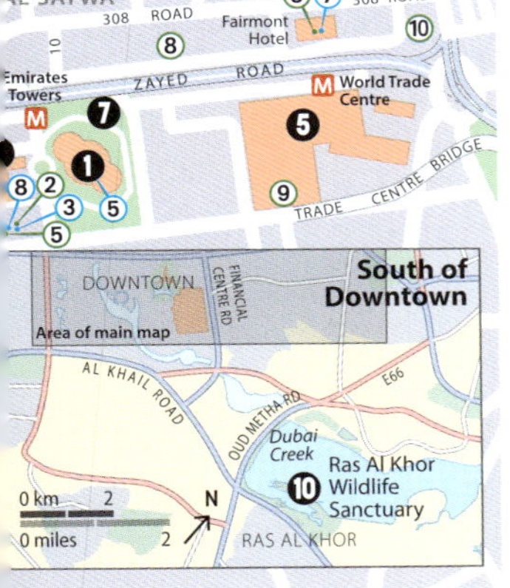

3 Burj Khalifa

C6 1 Sheikh Mohammed bin Rashid Blvd 8:30am–10pm daily burjkhalifa.ae

Named after the former UAE president Sheikh Khalifa bin Zayed Al Nahyan, the Burj Khalifa *(p22)* stands as the tallest building in the world. While much of the tower is residential, a pair of observation decks *(p23)* are open to visitors. At its base is the world's first Armani Hotel *(p22)*.

4 DIFC and the Gate

D6 Sheikh Zayed Rd difc.ae/experience/our-locations/gate-avenue

Behind the Emirates Towers is the Gate, a striking 15-storey architectural landmark at the heart of the Dubai International Financial Centre (DIFC). Shaped like a bridge, the Gate is designed to "bridge" the gap between the financial centres of London and New York in the West with Hong Kong and Tokyo in the East. Adjacent to this financial centre is the Gate Village, home to upscale art galleries.

5 Dubai World Trade Centre

E5 Sheikh Zayed Rd
dwtc.com

Although dwarfed today by the skyscrapers of Sheikh Zayed Road, the Dubai World Trade Centre (DWTC) was the tallest building in the city back in 1979, and was opened with great pomp by Sheikh Rashid and Queen Elizabeth II of the UK. It has played an important role in the city's development, a fact reflected by the continued use of its image on the AED 100 note. Today, the centre also comprises 14 huge exhibition halls. The Dubai International Convention Centre next door can accommodate more than 10,000.

6 Palace Downtown

C6 Sheikh Mohammed bin Rashid Blvd addresshotels.com

Tucked away behind Souk Al Bahar is the opulent Palace Downtown. The hotel's exquisite Arabian-style façade and palm-lined ornamental pool are sights in their own right, made all the more memorable by the hotel's incongruous juxtaposition with the futuristic Burj Khalifa rising directly behind. The hotel's Thiptara restaurant *(p79)* offers fine Thai dining and some peerless views of the Dubai Fountain.

GODOLPHIN

The famous Godolphin racing stable *(godolphin.com)* was established by the equestrian-loving Maktoum Royal Family of Dubai in 1994. It has won Group One races in 11 countries. It bred the great Dubai Millennium, who won the Dubai World Cup 2000 by over six lengths and sired 59 offspring.

7 Museum of the Future

E5 Sheikh Zayed Rd
10am–7:30pm daily
museumofthefuture.ae

This remarkable museum is an initiative of the Dubai Future Foundation, which sets out to explore the most pressing issues relating to humanity's collective future. Housed in a beautiful silver orb, the museum uses cutting-edge technologies to explore climate change, the future of artificial intelligence and new forms of social organization.

8 Souk Al Bahar

C6 Sheikh Mohammed bin Rashid Blvd soukalbahar.ae

Next to the futuristic Burj Khalifa is a slice of old, albeit newly built, Arabia. Souk Al Bahar is an Arabesque shopping mall with over 100 retail outlets, including independent boutiques, souvenir shops and antique stores. Along the souk's pleasant waterfront promenade there are several restaurants, cafés and lounge bars. This is

Palm trees lining the entrance to Palace Downtown

the perfect spot for a stroll before you attempt the shopping madness of the Dubai Mall, which is just a few minutes' walk away.

9 The Dubai Mall

C6 Next to the Burj Khalifa 10am–midnight Thu–Sat, 10am–10pm Sun–Wed thedubaimall.com

The ultimate shrine to consumerism, this mall has a vast array of shops and other attractions, including the Dubai Aquarium, an ice rink and a skeleton of a 150-million-year-old diplodocus dinosaur. Highlights include the Arabian-themed souk section and the ultra-chic Fashion Avenue. The selection of places to eat includes some nice alfresco spots overlooking the Dubai Fountain.

10 Ras Al Khor Wildlife Sanctuary

E2 Ras Al Khor 800 900 9am–4pm Sat–Thu

Pink flamingos, waders and other birds can be viewed on a marshy reserve at the inner end of Dubai Creek. This urban reserve has two hides: Flamingo and Mangrove. Both are fitted out with telescopes, binoculars and picture panels. Note, entry to the hides is free, but groups of ten or more require a permit.

Flock of flamingos at the Ras Al Khor Wildlife Sanctuary

A STROLL AMONG THE SKYSCRAPERS

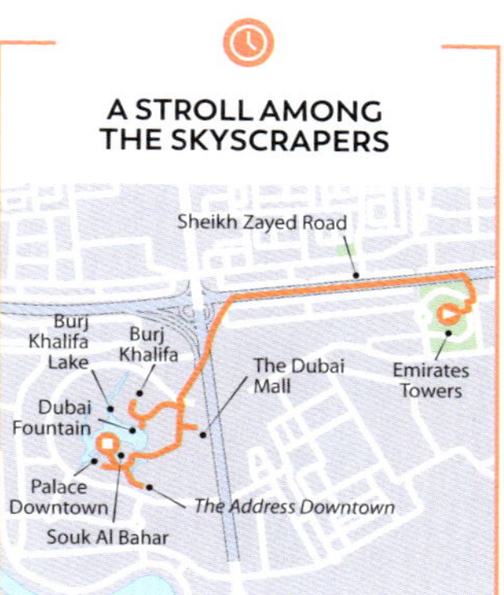

Morning

Begin with a stroll down **Sheikh Zayed Road**, starting at the **Emirates Towers** *(p74)* and admiring the many soaring skyscrapers here. Stop for breakfast in one of the cafés in **Souk Al Bahar** – Shakespeare and Co *(p53)* is popular for croissants and coffee. After breakfast, head to **The Dubai Mall** for shopping and enjoy exploring the Dubai Aquarium and the ice rink. Lunch at one of the cafés in the mall.

Afternoon

Next, return to the pretty, Arabian-themed **Souk Al Bahar**, where more shops await. Then pop into **Palace Downtown** for tea before a late-afternoon visit to the observation deck of the **Burj Khalifa** *(p75)* for Dubai's most amazing views (book ahead).

As dusk begins to fall, walk the promenade around **Burj Khalifa Lake** and watch the show-stopping **Dubai Fountain** *(p75)* spring into life. Next, head to **The Address Downtown** *(p23)* and enjoy a snack at the elegant lobby lounge offering gourmet sandwiches, scones and handpicked signature blends. Alternatively, head to the pan-Asian Karma Kafé *(p79)* in **Souk Al Bahar** or to one of the waterside restaurants for a sumptuous dinner.

Bars

1. Weslodge

A6 JW Marriott Marquis, Business Bay 5:30pm–2am daily weslodge.ae

A stylish, rock-and-roll-themed bar, known for its creative drinks and superb North American cuisine.

2. Avli by Tashas

D6 Unit C-01, Ground Floor, Gate Village Building 9 7pm–1am Sun–Wed avlibytashas.com

The popular Avli bar crafts creative cocktails inspired by the aromatic botanicals of the Cycladic islands.

3. Cin Cin

E5 Fairmont Hotel 7pm–3am daily fairmont.com

This chic champagne bar has a great snack menu offering freshly shucked oysters and Wagyu beef burgers.

4. The Balcony Bar

C5 Shangri-La Hotel 9am–2am daily shangri-la.com

An ideal place to unwind, this swanky restaurant overlooks the hotel's lobby. Enjoy drinks while soaking up the ambience.

5. Galaxy Bar

D6 Unit C-01, Ground Floor, Gate Village Building 9 8pm–3am Sun–Thu galaxy-bar.com

Ranked 45 on the World's 50 Best Bars in 2022, this glamorous bar serves excellent cocktails in the heart of fashionable DIFC.

6. Vault

B6 Business Bay 5pm–3am daily jwmarriottmarquisdubailife.com

One of the world's highest bars, Vault is located on the 72nd floor of the JW Marriott Marquis hotel. Svelte decor and a classy ambience complement the panoramic views.

Seats around the unusual circular bar area at Long's Bar

7. Long's Bar

D5 Towers Rotana Hotel Noon–3am daily rotana.com

This colonial-style bar, with its small dance floor, claims to have the longest bar in the whole of the UAE.

8. Fibber McGees

D5 Off Sheikh Zayed Rd 8am–2am daily fibbersdubai.com

Considered one of Dubai's best traditional pubs, this spot is tricky to find (check directions on the website) but definitely worth the effort. The homely interior will transport you straight to Ireland, as will the draught Kilkenny and Guinness. There's good food, too, plus regular live music.

9. Blue Bar

E5 Novotel World Trade Centre 04 310 8150 Noon–1am Mon–Thu, noon–2am Fri, 3pm–1am Sat & Sun

A low-key, relaxed bar where you can chill to the tunes of the resident band.

10. Miss Lily's

E5 Sheraton Grand Hotel 7pm–2am daily misslilys.com

A charming Caribbean bar with delightful house cocktails and spirits. The flavourful dishes served here draw from distinct Jamaican roots.

Places to Eat

1. Hoi An
C5 Shangri-La Hotel, Sheikh Zayed Rd 7pm–midnight daily (also 12:30–4pm Fri & Sat) shangri-la.com • DDD
Vietnamese fare served in elegant surroundings with a range of dishes and excellent service.

2. At.Mosphere
C6 122nd floor, Burj Khalifa Hours vary, call ahead atmosphereburjkhalifa.com • DDD
This place offers exceptional European-style fine dining on the 122nd floor of the Burj Khalifa.

3. Avli by Tashas
D6 Unit C-01, Ground Floor, Gate Village Building 9 Noon–4pm & 7pm–1am Sun–Wed avlibytashas.com • DDD
Dubai's most fashionable Greek restaurant, this is the best place to enjoy fine dining.

4. Karma Kafé
C6 Souk Al Bahar, Downtown Burj Khalifa Hours vary, check website karma-kafe.com • DD
Enjoy classic Asian fusion food in the plush interior or on the lovely terrace of this upscale Pan-Asian restaurant. The views of the nearby Burj Khalifa and Dubai Fountain are magnificent.

5. Ninive
E6 Emirates Towers Hotel 6pm–2am daily (to 3am Fri & Sat) ninive.ae • DD
One of the best Arabian restaurants in the city, Ninive offers mezze, grills and seafood in an open-air setting.

6. Teatro
D5 Towers Rotana Hotel 6pm–2am daily rotana.com • DD
The great cross-continental dishes here have made this restaurant a firm favourite for many years.

PRICE CATEGORIES

For a three-course meal for one with half a bottle of wine (or equivalent meal), taxes and extra charges.

D under AED 100 **DD** AED 100–400
DDD over AED 400

7. Opa
E5 FairmontHotel 7pm–2am daily opaworld.com • DDD
Opa serves traditional Greek cuisine in a Cyclades-inspired setting.

8. Zuma Dubai
D6 Dubai International Financial Centre Hours vary, check website zumarestaurant.com • DDD
This globally acclaimed Japanese restaurant offers *izakaya*-style dining with *robata* grills and sushi.

9. Le Petit Maison
D6 Dubai International Financial Centre 7–11am, noon–3pm & 7–11pm daily lpmrestaurants.com• DD
Reminiscent of the Côte d'Azur, this place has a delightful menu of French Mediterranean and Niçoise cuisine.

10. Thiptara
C6 Palace Downtown Hours vary, check website addresshotels.com • DDD
Set in a beautiful wooden pavilion on the lakeside, this venue specializes in Thai seafood. Book ahead.

Cosy table seating at Karma Kafé

JUMEIRAH

Stretching down the coast southwest from the port area, Jumeirah is one of the most glamorous and sought-after areas in Dubai, thanks to its quiet leafy streets and bougainvillea-clad luxury villas, which don't come cheap. At the southern end of the district the extensive low-rise suburbs are punctuated by three of the city's most famous landmarks: the iconic "seven-star" Jumeirah Burj Al Arab, the enormous wave-shaped Jumeirah Beach Hotel and the vast mock-Arabian Madinat Jumeirah complex (home to the beautiful Souk Madinat Jumeirah). As such, staying here is an expensive pleasure, which is added to by some of the city's finest beaches, bars and restaurants, located in the area. And for those energetic enough to leave the relaxing resorts for something more thrilling, the Wild Wadi Water Park offers fun thrills and spills.

Impressive Jumeirah Burj Al Arab, dominating the Jumeirah skyline

1 Jumeirah Burj Al Arab

Visible from almost anywhere in Jumeirah, the stunning Jumeirah Burj Al Arab *(p30)*, a luxury hotel, is a symbol of the city itself and is distinguished by its unusual shape mirroring the billowing sail of a *dhow*. Advance reservations are needed to visit the interior of this opulent hotel. For a great close-up view of the exterior, drop into the Jumeirah Beach Hotel and take the super-fast glass elevator to the top floor.

For places to stay in this area, see p115

2 Jumeirah Mosque

Rising proudly above Jumeirah Road, the imposing Fatimid-style Jumeirah Mosque *(p28)* is one of the city's most impressive and attractive mosques.

3 Ski Dubai Snow Park

C2 Mall of the Emirates 10am–midnight daily (from 9am Fri & Sat) skidxb.com

You can't miss Ski Dubai from the Sheikh Zayed Road, jutting out like a giant space-age tube. Filled with over 6,000 tonnes of snow, it offers five slopes, linked by chairlifts and tow lifts, to cater to all ski levels, including the longest black indoor run in the world. There's also a snow park for little ones, plus a set of thrilling rides and activities such as snowboarding.

4 Wild Wadi Water Park

C2 Jumeirah Rd Hours vary, check website wildwadi.com

This world-class water park offers a great day out to suit all ages and bravery levels, with 30 water-fuelled rides and attractions. Thrill-seekers will not be disappointed by its most challenging ride, Jumeirah Sceirah, the tallest and fastest freefall water slide outside the US. There's also the gravity-defying Master Blasters, a "water" coaster with jets that shoot riders 15 m (50 ft) up in the air, and Breaker's Bay, the Middle East's largest wave pool. The park is well staffed with experienced lifeguards and has plenty of food outlets.

Relaxing in the pool at the Wild Wadi Water Park

5 Safa Park

A5

Created in 1975, Safa is Dubai's first public park. This lush expanse stretches from Al Wasl Road to Sheikh Zayed Road, which cuts through by the meandering Dubai Water Canal, an extension of Dubai Creek. The park is popular with local residents, many of whom make the most of its specially sprung perimeter jogging track. It's great for kids to run free and there's lots of entertainment, including a mini-train, a merry-go-round and a lake with rowing boats. A ride on the Ferris wheel here offers the best view of the beautifully landscaped surroundings.

6 Madinat Jumeirah

C2 Al Sufouh Rd

This vast leisure and entertainment complex is a major focus of the Jumeirah area. It has three hotels linked by waterways navigated by silent battery-powered *abras*. There are numerous restaurants, bars and cafés, many with great waterside views, with the seafood restaurant Pierchic *(p85)* located on a pier that stretches into the Arabian Gulf. Also located here is the Souk Madinat Jumeirah *(p84)*, a reconstruction of a traditional Arabian bazaar.

Traditional *abras* at Madinat Jumeirah

JUMEIRAH'S BEACHES AND DUBAI'S BEACH CULTURE

All of the hotels in Jumeirah are fronted by their own private stretches of golden beach onto the Arabian Gulf, but there are plenty of public beaches too, which fill up at weekends. There are also family-friendly beach parks with a small entrance charge: the best in this area is the Jumeirah Beach Park.

7 Mall of the Emirates

C2 Interchange 4

malloftheemirates.com

Dubai's swankiest retail complex has more than 500 shops and department stores, selling every product you can possibly dream of. For those who don't want to shop, the mall has plenty of other attractions, including a multi-screen cinema and kids' play area, Magic Planet, plus dozens of cafés and restaurants.

8 Jumeirah Beach Park

A4

This lovely green park backs onto a beautiful white-sand beach. You can access the beach from the park along wooden walkways and there is plenty of shade on the sand under

Palm-fringed white sands of Jumeirah Beach Park

the palm trees. It's equipped with lifeguards, and has good facilities. Some small cafés are also lined along the beach.

9 Al Quoz Galleries

C2 alserkalavenue.ae

The gritty industrial area of Al Quoz has been transformed by the cutting-edge art galleries that have moved into the area. Many local galleries are relocating into the Alserkal Avenue arts centre on Street 8, including leading names like Efie Gallery *(p44)* and Green Art Gallery *(p45)*.

10 Majlis Ghorfat Um Al Sheef

D2 17 St 800 33222
7:30am–3:30pm Mon–Fri

Hidden among the suburban sprawl, the Majlis Ghorfat Um Al Sheef is the only historic building to survive outside the old city centre. Built in 1955, this quaint two-storey structure served as a summer retreat for visionary former ruler Sheikh Rashid, with sleeping quarters below and a *majlis* (meeting room) above. The garden has date palm trees watered using traditional *falaj* irrigation channels.

A DAY BY THE SEA

Morning

Start your day with an insightful morning tour of the **Jumeirah Mosque** *(p28)*, one of Dubai's finest Islamic buildings. Then, drive or hire a taxi to **Jumeirah Beach Park**, where you can swim or laze under the palm trees. Leave at lunchtime and head to **Madinat Jumeirah**, where you can enjoy a leisurely late lunch at a huge choice of restaurants, many overlooking the waterways.

Afternoon

Afterwards spend an hour or two window-shopping for souvenirs or browsing the lovely Arabian-style **Souk Madinat Jumeirah** *(p84)* here.

As evening approaches, head to one of Dubai's most beautiful bars, the **Bahri Bar** *(p85)*, housed in the luxurious Mina Al Salam hotel. From this beautiful alfresco spot, you can sip a cocktail while enjoying superb views of the **Jumeirah Burj Al Arab** *(p80)* and watching the sun set over the Gulf. There are numerous places to eat dinner nearby, but for the most romantic experience, head to the delectable Pai Thai in the nearby **Dar al Masyaf** hotel *(jumeirah.com/en/stay)*. With fine Thai cuisine in a magical setting, which overlooks the meandering waterways of the Medinat and the Burj, a meal here is hard to beat. It is recommended to book in advance.

Opulent complex of Souk Madinat Jumeirah

Places to Shop

1. Mall of the Emirates
Prepare to shop until you drop at one of the biggest shopping centres *(p82)* in the region.

2. Camel Company
C2 Souk Madinat Jumeirah
10am–11pm daily camelcompany.ae
Dubai's cutest selection of cuddly toy camels and other dromedary-themed souvenirs – perfect for kids.

3. Times Square Center
C2 Sheikh Zayed Rd 10am–10pm daily (to midnight Fri & Sat)
timessquarecenter.ae
This mall features an impressive electronics store. It also has an ice lounge where everything, from the tables to the glasses, is made of ice.

4. The Village Mall
D4 Jumeirah Rd 04 344 9514
10am–10pm daily (from 2pm Fri)
An intriguing mix of niche upmarket boutiques fills this pretty shopping centre, with its archways, plants and fountains. It is the perfect place to find a one-of-a-kind gift.

5. Gallery One
C2 Souk Madinat Jumeirah
10am–11pm daily g-1.com
This commercial gallery specializes in selling beautiful but relatively affordable limited-edition Arabian- and Asian-themed artworks.

6. Souk Madinat Jumeirah
C2 Al Sufouh Rd
10am–11pm daily
This magical bazaar has art, jewellery, antiques and handicrafts, interspersed with great bars and restaurants.

7. Boxpark
D2 Al Wasl Rd 10am–midnight Thu–Sat, 10am–10pm Sun–Wed
boxpark.ae
A funky retail space made up of minimalist cuboid buildings with the odd shipping container poking out, housing eclectic and offbeat shops.

8. Pride of Kashmir
C2 Souk Madinat Jumeirah
10am–11pm daily prideofkashmir.com
A craft and souvenir shop packed with antique and modern rugs from Iran, Kashmir and Turkey.

9. Mercato Mall
C4 Jumeirah Beach Rd
10am–10pm daily mercatoshoppingmall.com
An Italian-themed mall with 90 shops, restaurants and cafés. With a fun soft play area, it is great for kids.

10. Jumeirah Plaza
D4 Jumeirah Rd 04 349 0766
10am–10pm daily (from 1:30pm Fri)
This small mall, popular with local residents, has a pleasant coffee shop with an outdoor terrace.

Places to Eat

PRICE CATEGORIES

For a three-course meal for one with half a bottle of wine (or equivalent meal), taxes and extra charges.

D under AED 100 **DD** AED 100–400
DDD over AED 400

1. COYA Dubai

D4 Four Seasons Resort
Hours vary, check website
coyarestaurant.com · DD

Exquisite Peruvian dishes fused with Japanese, Chinese and Spanish elements are on offer at this venue.

2. Zheng He's

C2 Jumeirah Mina Al Salam
Noon–3pm & 6:30–11:30pm daily
jumeirah.com · DDD

Dine on fresh seafood and Chinese cuisine by the harbourfront.

3. Trattoria

C2 Madinat Jumeirah 800 323 232 Noon–midnight daily · DD

Delicious Italian fare is served in a mock Venetian waterway setting.

4. Pierchic

C1 Al Qasr 12:30–3pm daily (also 6:15pm–midnight Sat & Sun) jumeirah.com · DDD

Book a terrace table at this seafood restaurant on a wooden pier.

5. Orfali Bros

D4 Wasl 51 Mall, Jumeirah 1
Noon–midnight daily
orfalibros.com · DD

The Syrian Orfali brothers' excellent Levantine dishes have earned them the top spot in the Middle East and North Africa's 50 Best Restaurants.

6. Maria Bonita's Taco Shop

C2 Umm Al Sheif St Noon–midnight daily mariabonitatacoshop.com · D

Be transported to Mexico with some good-value tacos, tortillas and salsas.

7. Sho Cho's

E4 Dubai Marine Beach Resort and Spa Hours vary, check website
sho-cho.com · DD

This super-chic Japanese bar-café has a gorgeous terrace overlooking the Gulf.

8. Hoseki

D2 Bulgari Resort, Jumeirah 2 1–11pm Wed–Sun bulgarihotels.com · DDD

A Michelin-starred restaurant serving exquisite Japanese food by chef Masahiro Sugiyama. The *omakase*-style tasting menus feature fresh catches from Tokyo.

9. Nusr-Et Steakhouse

D4 Four Seasons Resort
Hours vary, check website
nusr-et.com.tr · DD

A unique restaurant founded by the internet sensation chef Nusret Gökçe, known popularly as Salt Bae. It celebrates the tradition of Turkish-style steakhouses and has a superb menu.

10. Bahri Bar

C2 Jumeirah Mina Al Salam, Madinat Jumeirah 800 323 232
4pm–2am daily · DD

With a large terrace offering great views of the Jumeirah Burj Al Arab light shows, this is an ideal spot for a sundowner and light bites.

Plush seating at the Bahri Bar

DUBAI MARINA AND PALM JUMEIRAH

Thirty years ago, this area south of the historic centre was little more than empty desert and open sea, with a few isolated developments hinting at the city's ambitions. Today, it has been transformed into a glittering residential and tourist destination. The Dubai Marina neighbourhood stretches along the Arabian Sea coastline, backed by shining towers that create a dramatic high-rise skyline. At its heart is a chic marina filled with gleaming yachts and surrounded by stylish cafés, restaurants and promenades. Beyond the skyscrapers, a wide swathe of golden beach is lined with stunning luxury resorts, drawing visitors and residents in droves. Just offshore lies the Palm Jumeirah, the world's largest human-made island, shaped like a giant palm tree and crowned at its far end by the iconic Atlantis, The Palm resort and the newer Atlantis The Royal.

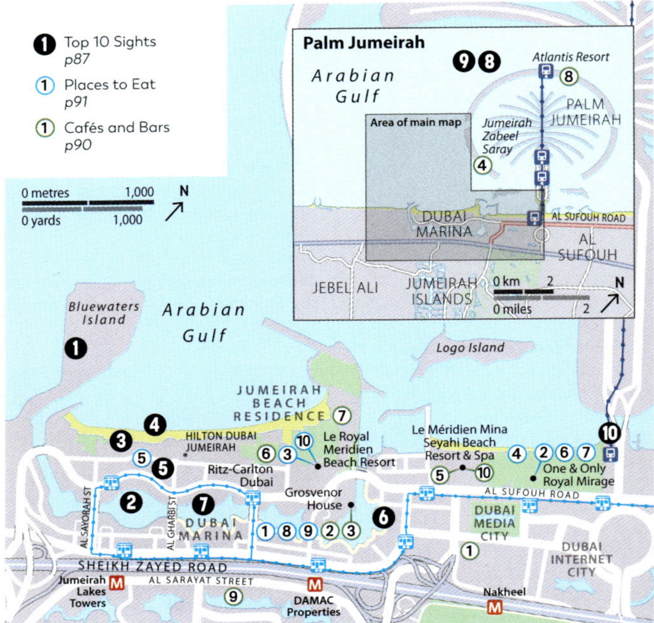

For places to stay in this area, see p116

1 Bluewaters Island

B1

At the end of Jumeirah Beach Residence, connected via a picturesque footbridge, is the Bluewaters Island development, which is home to the Ain Dubai (Dubai Eye) *(p32)*, the world's tallest Ferris wheel. The wheel offers incredible views over the waterfront, and each capsule is fitted with LCD screens which point out prominent structures on the skyline. On the island, there are also several trendy restaurants and bars, including Chinese den Shi and the London Project. Explore the wealth of attractions here, or simply spend the day chilling at Cove Beach Club.

2 Dubai Marina

B2

Centrepiece of the Dubai Marina development is the expansive marina itself, lined with millionaires' boats and surrounded by skyscrapers on all sides. It is particularly impressive when illuminated after dark. Created out of a human-made sea inlet running parallel to the ocean, the marina is the best part of the 3-km- (2-mile-) long shoreline. Disorientated sharks and even whales have been known to swim into it from time to time.

Admiring Dubai's stunning skyline from Ain Dubai

3 The Beach at JBR

This lovely stretch of white sand *(p32)* is one of the marina's top attractions and the best free beach in the city. The size of the beach means that there's usually plenty of space to lounge on (although it does get busy, particularly at weekends), and there are facilities such as showers and changing rooms, plus loungers for hire. This is also the best place for water sports, with varied activities, including sailing, kayaking, water-skiing and boating.

4 AquaFun Dubai Water Park

B1 Jumeirah Beach Residences 9am–sunset daily aquafun.ae

The world's largest inflatable water park, AquaFun is an obstacle course of slippery wet slides and tubes. The challenge is to not slip and fall into the water. It's much harder than it looks and provides great fun for all the family.

Luxury boats and towering skyscrapers, Dubai Marina

5 The Walk at JBR

B2

Running along the beachfront is the Walk at JBR, a long boulevard of shops, restaurants, cafés and hotels backed by the huge towers of the Jumeirah Beach Residence, which is one of the city's most relaxed places for an outdoor stroll. Adjacent, the Beach at JBR *(p32)* is among Dubai's most attractive recent developments, with a low-rise cluster of shops and restaurants around pretty piazzas and fountains.

6 Marina Walk

B2

Encircling both sides of Dubai Marina is the pedestrianized Marina Walk. An array of cafés and restaurants line the waterfront here, along with the swanky Marina Mall. At the northern end of the marina, look out for the unmistakeable 73-storey Cayan Tower with its remarkable twisted shape – the entire building rotates over 90 degrees. Across the road, the new Dubai Harbour development now welcomes gleaming cruise ships, which tower over the superyachts.

7 Boat Trips at the Marina

The marina development is best appreciated from the water, and there are a range of boat trips available to make this possible. The cheapest and simplest option is to take a ride on one of the water taxis, which shuttle up and down the marina itself, and there are also after-dark dinner cruises aboard traditional *dhows*. Alternatively, catch a ride on the Dubai Ferry *(p107)* that runs between Bur Dubai and the marina or go for a sightseeing tour with the Yellow Boats *(p59)*.

8 Aquaventure

B1 Atlantis, The Palm 10am–sunset atlantisthepalm.com

The Aquaventure water park offers state-of-the-art rides and attractions. The highlight is the huge Leap of Faith slide, which lands you in a transparent tunnel through a shark-filled lagoon. Guests staying at Atlantis, The Palm and the nearby Atlantis, The Royal have complimentary access to the thrilling water park. Visitors can purchase tickets to the park through the website.

Underwater-themed interior of Atlantis, The Palm

9 Atlantis, The Palm

Dominating the far end of the Palm Jumeirah is the vast Atlantis, The Palm resort *(p116)*. This is one of the city's most distinctive landmarks, a soaring pink colossus arranged around a vast Arabian-style archway. The resort's lavish interior is a riot of golden columns and marble floors. Nearby attractions include Aquaventure and a vast swathe of delightfully golden beach.

10 Palm Monorail

B1–B2 10am–10pm daily
palm-monorail.com

The only place you really get a proper view of the Palm Jumeirah is from the air. If your budget can't quite stretch to a helicopter ride, the Palm Monorail offers the best overview of the development, running on a raised track across the island and offering great views of the Palm and the towering skyscrapers of the Dubai Marina in the distance. Trains depart every 20 to 30 minutes.

Enjoying a trip down the lazy river at Aquaventure

A DAY ON LAND AND OUT AT SEA

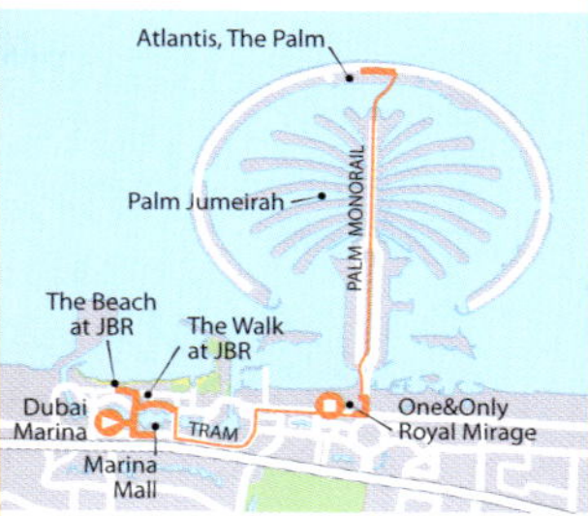

Morning

Start with a pleasant stroll around **Dubai Marina** *(p87)*. Spend some time exploring the **Marina Mall** or take a boat trip. Next, walk to the nearby **The Beach at JBR** *(p32)*. Take some time in the sun or maybe try one of the water sports on offer here. Afterwards, explore the shops along **The Walk at JBR** and grab lunch in one of the many cafés and restaurants here.

Afternoon

After lunch, catch the Dubai tram to Palm Monorail station and ride the **Palm Monorail** to **Atlantis, The Palm**, with bird's-eye views of the **Palm Jumeirah** on the way. Admire the lavish interior and visit some of the resort's attractions.

Evening

Hop back on the monorail to the mainland. From Palm Monorail station continue to the nearby **One&Only Royal Mirage**. Spend an enjoyable evening admiring the hotel's magical Moorish architecture and endless palm trees. Start with a drink at Moroccan-style The Rooftop terrace bar, followed by dinner at one of the resort's excellent restaurants. The pool-fringed Eauzone *(p91)* is particularly romantic, but you will need to book ahead.

Cafés and Bars

Terrace bar at Siddharta Lounge by Buddha-Bar

1. Jato

B2 Media One, Dubai Media City 5pm–1am daily jato.ae

Located on the 43rd floor of Media One hotel, this Peruvian hotspot offers daily happy hours and a ladies' night on Tuesday.

2. Siddharta Lounge by Buddha-Bar

B2 Grosvenor House Dubai, Al Emreef St, Dubai Marina 6pm–1am daily (to 2am Fri & Sat) siddhartalounge.com

Siddharta Lounge by Buddha-Bar combines a beautiful boho restaurant with an outdoor terrace bar.

3. Bar 44

B2 Grosvenor House Dubai, Al Emreef St, Dubai Marina 4pm–2am daily (to 3am Thu) bar44-dubai.com

This top-floor swanky bar with comfy sofas and a giant balcony offers 44 different types of champagne.

4. The Jetty Lounge

B2 One&Only Royal Mirage, Al Sufouh 04 399 9999 5pm–1am daily

Known for its sunset views, this chic beachfront lounge offers Mediterranean bites and sundowners . It's the ideal spot for alfresco winter evenings by the sea.

5. ATTIKO High Energy Lounge

B2 W Dubai – Mina Seyahi, Dubai Marina 5pm–2am daily (to 3am Fri & Sat) theattiko.com

Inspired by cosmopolitan Asian nightclubs, ATTIKO enjoys 31st-floor views over the Dubai Harbour development and Palm Jumeirah.

6. Caña by Tamoka

B2 Ritz-Carlton Dubai, JBR The Walk, Dubai Marina Noon–10pm daily tamokadubai.com

Located on the beach in front of Tamoka Dubai restaurant, this tiny beach hut bar serves great cocktails.

7. Zero Gravity

B1 Al Sufouh Rd Hours vary, check website 0-gravity.ae

This beachfront bar-restaurant is a lovely place to linger over a sundowner.

8. Cloud 22

B1 Atlantis, The Royal, Crescent Rd, Palm Jumeirah 10am–dusk daily atlantis.com/atlantis-the-royal

Cloud 22 is exclusively open to guests of Atlantis, The Royal *(p116)* and it's worth booking a room just to experience it.

9. Nola

B2 Armada BlueBay Hotel, Cluster P, JLT Noon–3am daily nola-social.com

A New Orleans-inspired bar with a lovely ambience. Book ahead.

10. Barasti

B2 Le Meridien Mina Seyahi Beach Resort and Marina 10am–3:30am daily barastibeach.com

Barasti comes alive at the weekends, when revellers sprawl out across the sand. There is live music most nights.

Places to Eat

1. Pitfire Pizza

B2 Lake Terrace Tower, Cluster D 11am–11pm daily pitfirepizza bakers.com · DD

One of Dubai's best pizza restaurants serves a wide array of traditional and innovative pizzas.

2. Tagine

B2 One&Only Royal Mirage, Al Sufouh 7–11:30pm Tue–Sun oneandonlyresorts.com · DD

Visit this candlelit restaurant for a magical Moroccan experience. The courtyard location adds to its charm.

3. Maya

B2 Le Royal Meridien Beach Resort 7pm–1am Sat–Wed, 7pm–2am Thu, 12:30–4pm & 7pm–2am Sun maya-dubai.com · DDD

Experience new-wave Mexican cuisine in spacious surroundings decorated with Mayan art and modern sculpture.

4. Amala

B1 Jumeirah Zabeel Saray, Palm Jumeirah 1–4pm & 6–11:30pm daily jumeirah.com · DD

Enjoy tasty North Indian dishes in a lavish setting with traditional décor.

5. BiCE

B2 Hilton Dubai Jumeirah 12:30–3:30pm & 7–11:30pm bicemare.com · DD

This Art Deco-themed Italian restaurant has an excellent selection of seafood, meat dishes and wine.

6. Eauzone

B2 One&Only Royal Mirage, Al Sufouh Noon–3:30pm & 7–11:30pm oneandonlyresorts.com · DDD

Enjoy classic Pan-Asian dishes and contemporary fine-dining creations here under tented canopies.

PRICE CATEGORIES

For a three-course meal for one with half a bottle of wine (or equivalent meal), taxes and extra charges.

D under AED 100 **DD** AED 100–400 **DDD** over AED 400

7. Trèsind

B2 One&Only Royal Mirage, Al Sufouh 12:30–3:30pm & 6:30–11pm daily tresind.com · DDD

Sample sophisticated Indian cuisine in a charming setting. The menu is created by the acclaimed chef Himanshu Saini.

8. Indego by Vineet

B2 Grosvenor House Dubai, Al Emreef St, Dubai Marina 7–11:30pm daily indegobyvineet.com · DDD

A contemporary take on traditional Indian cuisine overseen by chef Vineet Bhatia, the first Indian chef to be awarded a Michelin star.

9. City Social

B2 Grosvenor House, Dubai Al Emreef St, Dubai Marina 6pm–2am daily (to 3am Fri & Sat) city socialdubai.com · DD

Celebrity chef Jason Atherton's latest Dubai restaurant serves elevated British comfort food.

10. Rhodes Twenty10

B2 Le Royal Méridien Beach Resort 7pm–midnight rhodestwenty10.com · DDD

This stylish restaurant features a mix of British classics and Middle Eastern-influenced dishes.

Moroccan-inspired décor at Tagine

DOWNTOWN ABU DHABI

A stunning city of shiny new skyscrapers lining an idyllic corniche, oil-rich Abu Dhabi is the capital of the UAE and a rising player in the world's financial, commercial and tourist stages. After spending years in the shadow of neighbouring Dubai, Abu Dhabi launched its own spate of large-scale developments, ranging from the ultra-opulent Arabian-style Emirates Palace, one of the world's most lavish hotels, to the futuristic architecture of Al Maryah Island and the gleaming Etihad Towers. Downtown Abu Dhabi is the city's bustling commercial centre, with the biggest developments, the liveliest attractions, and the busiest shops, bars and restaurants.

Towering skyscrapers at Al Maryah Island

1 Al Maryah Island

T3

Located on the northern side of Downtown Abu Dhabi, this island is the site of arguably the city's most ambitious mega-project. Abu Dhabi's new financial and business district, the island is home to Abu Dhabi Global

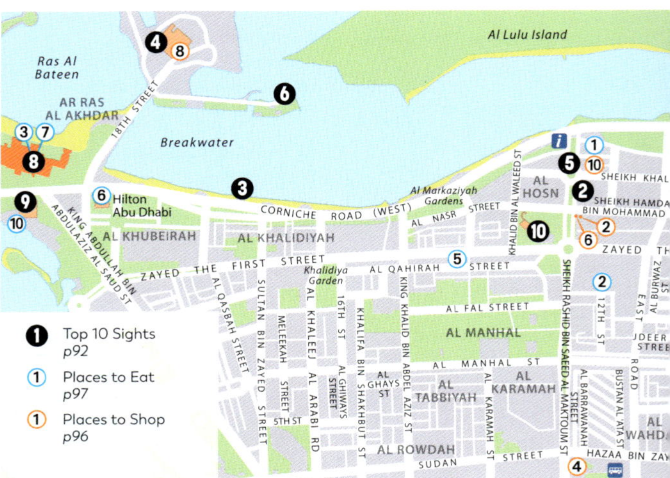

For places to stay in this area, see p116

Strolling along the Abu Dhabi Corniche

Market Square, a Four Seasons and a Rosewood hotel, the city's largest IMAX cinema and the chic Galleria mall *(p96)*.

2 World Trade Centre

R2 Hamdan Bin Mohammed St wtcad.ae

One of the largest developments in Abu Dhabi, the World Trade Centre is topped by the Burj Mohammed bin Rashid and the Trust Tower. The main attraction is its souk *(p96)*– a postmodern reimagining of a traditional Arabian souk.

3 Abu Dhabi Corniche

N1–R1

Abu Dhabi's showpiece boulevard sweeps for almost 5 km (3 miles) along the Downtown waterfront. A long line of skyscrapers rises to one side, while to the other is a series of gardens, popular in the evenings with strolling locals and joggers. Hiring a bike and riding up and down the waterfront is a great way to spend an hour or so, and there's a fine stretch of public beach.

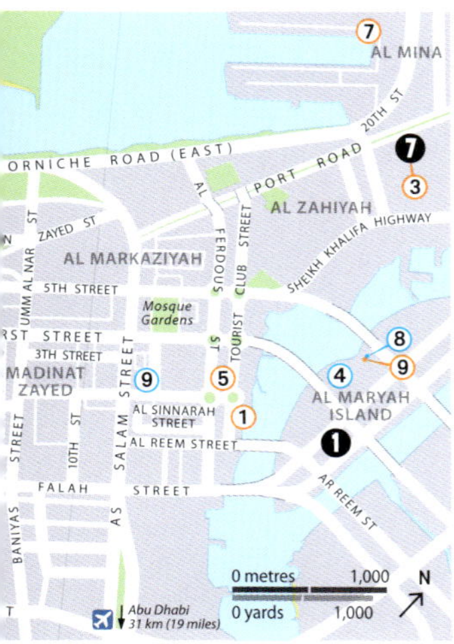

4 Marina Mall

P1 The Breakwater 10am–10pm daily (to midnight Thu & Fri) marina mall.ae

Despite its slightly out-of-the way location, the sprawling Marina Mall is one of the city's largest and most popular shopping destinations, with shops laid out between an attractive sequence of circular atriums topped with tent-shaped roofs. The highlight of the complex is the slender Marina Sky Tower, at the back of the mall, which offers superb views over the city and Corniche from the Colombiano coffee shop (Floor 41) or the Tiara revolving restaurant (Floor 42).

5 Al Ittihad Square

R1

A crop of supersized sculptures stand in the small park at the centre of Al Ittihad Square, creating a whimsical contrast to the surrounding tower blocks. The five sculptures feature a gigantic coffeepot, a huge perfume bottle, an elaborate plate cover, a colossal cannon and a small fort.

6 Abu Dhabi Heritage Village

P1 The Breakwater 9am–4pm Sat–Thu, 3:30–9pm Fri visitabudhabi.ae

For a taste of life in the city before the discovery of oil, visit Abu Dhabi's Heritage Village. Located over the water, across from the soaring towers of the Corniche, the village comprises a line of traditional *barasti* (palm-frond) huts, some of them turned into workshops in which resident craftspeople may be seen at work.

THE DISCOVERY OF OIL

The Japanese invention of the cultured pearl and the subsequent collapse of the Gulf's pearl industry led to the granting of petroleum concessions by Sheikh Shakhbut bin Sultan Al Nahyan in 1939. It turned out to be a very wise move. The discovery of oil in 1958 and its export from 1962 made Abu Dhabi an extremely rich city.

7 Al Mina Souks

V2 Al Mina 5am–11pm daily

Stretching away on the northern side of Downtown Abu Dhabi is the Al Mina port area with a trio of small markets. The so-called Carpet Souk *(p96)* here comprises a small square with low-key shops. The nearby food souk is the heart of the city's retail in vegetables and fruit, while opposite is the lively fish market, displaying the day's catch.

8 Emirates Palace

N1 West Corniche Rd emiratespalace.com

Abu Dhabi's magnificent pink palace hotel dominates the western end of the splendid Corniche. The majestic multi-domed exterior is surpassed in extravagance only by the dazzling interior which glitters with gold and sparkles with Swarovski crystals. The palace was constructed to provide opulent accommodation fitting for the capital's visiting dignitaries.

9 Etihad Towers

N2 King Abdullah Bin Abdulaziz Al Saud St 10am–6pm daily etihadtowers.com

Dominating the southwestern end of the Corniche is the huge Etihad Towers development, a cluster of five glistening skyscrapers with

gently curved outlines and a gleaming metallic shine. There are superlative views over Abu Dhabi from the 74th-floor Observation Deck at 300 (in tower two) and from Ray's Bar on the 62nd floor of the Jumeirah at Etihad Towers hotel.

10 Qasr al Hosn

R2 Al Nasr St (5th St)
qasralhosn.ae

Located at the heart of Downtown, Qasr al Hosn (the Palace Fort) offers an unexpected throwback to earlier times. This is the oldest building in Abu Dhabi, first constructed back in the 1760s, following which it served as home to the ruling Al Nahyan family for the next two centuries. Visitors can also see the development of Abu Dhabi as a metropolis. Most of what you see now – a high white wall dotted with a sequence of circular battlemented towers – was built in the 1940s. A highlight is the House of Artisans, where local crafts are explored through interactive workshops that teach traditions from basket weaving to embroidery.

Stunning Emirates Palace near to the Corniche

A CORNICHE AND CITY WALK

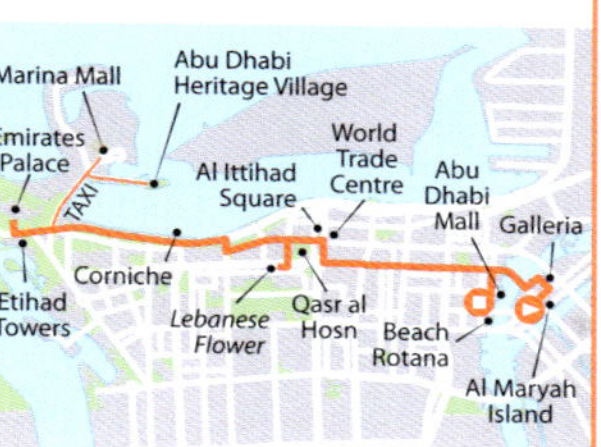

Morning

Start with a stroll around the stunning Abu Dhabi Global Market Square (Sowwah Square) on **Al Maryah Island** (*p92*) and explore the boutiques of **The Galleria** (*p96*). Then, head along the waterfront before crossing the bridge to the Downtown area. Wander past the **Abu Dhabi Mall** (*p96*) and along 5th St, one of the city's liveliest shopping areas, then check out the souk at the **World Trade Center** (*p96*) and admire the quirky statues in **Al Ittihad Square** (*p93*). From here, it's a short stroll past **Qasr al Hosn** for lunch at the **Lebanese Flower** restaurant (*p97*).

Afternoon

Walk down past Al Markaziyah Gardens to the spectacular **Corniche** (*p93*) and then stroll along a bit of the waterfront before taking a cab past the **Etihad Towers** for afternoon tea in the opulent surroundings of the **Emirates Palace** hotel. Catch another cab for the short drive to the **Abu Dhabi Heritage Village**. You can watch the sun set from the top of the Sky Tower in the **Marina Mall** (*p93*).

Catch a taxi back to Downtown and enjoy the nighttime view of Al Maryah Island from the terrace of the Finz restaurant at the **Beach Rotana** hotel (*p46*). End the day with a drink at the hotel's German-themed Brauhaus pub.

Alfresco dining at the sprawling Marina Mall

Places to Shop

1. Abu Dhabi Mall

T2 Tourist Club area 10am–10pm daily (to 11pm Thu & Fri) abudhabi-mall.com

Known as "AD Mall", this popular spot has all the top-name shops.

2. Fotouh Al Khair Mall

R2 Airport Rd 10am–10pm daily fotouhalkhairmall.com

Expats love this bright mini mall. It is home to Marks & Spencer and a number of other popular UK brands.

3. Carpet Souk

U2 Mina (Port) Rd

This souk is more about the buying experience than the items on offer (carpets, rugs, kilims and cushions).

4. Al Wahda Mall

R3 Near Central Bus Stop 10am–11pm Thu–Sat, 10am–10pm Sun–Wed alwahda-mall.com

With more than 250 stores and a cinema hall, this recently expanded mall is now the largest in Abu Dhabi.

5. Khalifa Centre

T2 10th St, opposite Abu Dhabi Mall, Tourist Club area 02 667 9900 10am–1pm & 4–10pm daily

Bargain here for exquisite Persian rugs, sheeshas, tribal kilims and even silver prayer boxes.

6. Hamdan St

R2 Sheikh Hamdan bin Mohammed St (Hamdan St)

This street sells almost everything. It has jewellery stores and Arabic and Bollywood music shops, as well as discount supermarkets.

7. Iranian Souq

U2 Mina (Port) Rd

Amid the plastic items and plants sold here, you'll find Iranian painted crafts.

8. Marina Mall

This enormous mall *(p93)* is packed with stores, cinemas and cafés. There is even an ice rink.

9. The Galleria

T2 Al Maryah Island 10am–10pm daily (to midnight Thu & Fri) thegalleria.ae

Spanning three floors, the Galleria houses numerous luxury boutique stores from across the world.

10. World Trade Center Souk

R2 Off Al Ittihad Square 10am–10pm daily (to 11pm Thu & Fri) wtcad.ae

Explore craft and souvenir shops at this stunning souk within the World Trade Center *(p93)*. You can also buy local food, spices and honey here.

Places to Eat

1. Pickl

R2 World Trade Centre 11am–2am daily (to 3am Fri & Sat) eat pickl.com · D

Homegrown burger joint Pickl is famous for its juicy burgers and its special secret sauce. Vegan options are also available.

2. Beijing

R2 Madinat Zayed 11am–midnight daily taogroup.com · D

This popular spot goes above and beyond to prove that delicious Chinese food need not be costly.

3. Hakkasan Abu Dhabi

N1 Emirates Palace Mandarin Oriental, Corniche Rd West 6pm–midnight daily (noon–3pm Fri & Sat) mandarinoriental.com · DDD

Enjoy award-winning Cantonese staples in a building designed by French interior designers Gilles and Boissier.

4. Zuma Abu Dhabi

V2 Al Maryah Island Hours vary, check website zuma restaurant.com · DD

This spot serves superb Japanese fare with a wide selection of dishes from the kitchen, *robata* grill, and sushi counter.

5. Lebanese Flower

P3 Near Choitrams Supermarket, cnr Hamdan & Fourth St, Khalidya 8am–2am daily · D

A must-visit restaurant offering mezze (Arabic appetizers), smoky mixed grilled meat plates and honey-soaked baklava.

PRICE CATEGORIES

For a three-course meal for one with half a bottle of wine (or equivalent meal), taxes and extra charges.

D under AED 100 **DD** AED 100–400 **DDD** over AED 400

6. Vasco's

N2 Hilton Abu Dhabi, Corniche Rd West 02 681 1900 Noon–3:30pm & 7pm–11pm daily · DDD

This smart restaurant offers an amazing blend of European and Asian influences.

7. Sand & Koal

N1 Emirates Palace Mandarin Oriental, Corniche Rd West 5pm–1am daily (from 1pm Sat & from 3pm Sun) mandarinoriental.com · DDD

The beachfront Sand & Koal offers a dinner-and-theatre experience, with food cooked over an open-fire grill.

8. Royal Orchid

T2 The Galleria, Al Maryah Island Noon–11:30pm daily theroyal orchidgroup.com · D

This traditional Thai restaurant has a great atmosphere. Note, alcohol is not served here.

9. India Palace

T2 Al Salam St Noon–midnight daily indiapalace.ae · D

Enjoy North Indian cuisine in an opulent Anglo-Indian setting (alcohol not served).

10. Sushisamba Abu Dhabi

P2 Conrad Abu Dhabi Etihad Towers, Corniche Rd West 6pm–1am daily (to 2am Thu–Sat) sushisamba.com · DDD

Sushisamba has two colourful floors of Japanese, Brazilian and Peruvian culture and cuisine.

Outdoor seating at Hakkasan Abu Dhabi

BEYOND ABU DHABI

Beyond the central Downtown area, Abu Dhabi is booming. Beautiful beach-lined Saadiyat Island, a couple of miles east from the centre, is home to Louvre Abu Dhabi (a sister museum to the Louvre in Paris) and contemporary art gallery Manarat Al Saadiyat. The Guggenheim Abu Dhabi, Zayed National Museum and Natural History Museum will soon be new additions, cementing the destination's status as a cultural hub. Past here, adjacent Yas Island is where you will find the city's famous Formula 1 racetrack and swanky Yas Marina, with the vast Ferrari World and Yas Waterworld theme parks close by. Back towards the centre, the city shows its more traditional side at the stunning Sheikh Zayed Mosque, one of the world's most spectacular modern mosques.

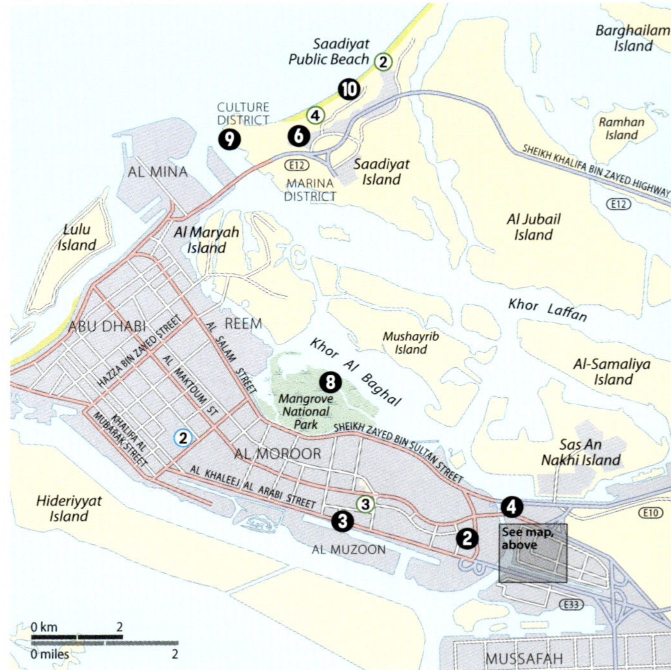

For places to stay in this area, see p117

Intricately detailed pillars, Sheikh Zayed Grand Mosque

1 Yas Island

Named for the Arabian Ban Yasi tribe, Yas Island *(p38)* is a premier Emirati leisure island and the official home of Formula 1 in Abu Dhabi, with the race held at the Yas Marina Circuit *(p39)*. It features the world's only hotel built over an F1 racetrack, the W Abu Dhabi *(p117)*, alongside popular attractions like the Ferrari World theme park *(p38)*. The island offers a range of experiences, from thrilling rides at Yas Waterworld *(p48)* to exciting shopping sprees.

2 Sheikh Zayed Grand Mosque

This impressive mosque *(p36)* is named after Sheikh Zayed bin Sultan Al Nahyan, the founder and the first president of the United Arab Emirates, who is also buried here. The building is open to non-Muslims, but visitors should dress appropriately.

3 Capital Gate

U3 Al Khaleej al Arabi St

The so-called "Leaning Tower of Abu Dhabi", Capital Gate is one of the most remarkable of Abu Dhabi's many strange modern buildings. Officially recognized by Guinness World Records as the world's most tilted tower, this enormous skyscraper looks as if it's on the point of toppling headfirst into the sea, with four times more lean than even the famously wonky Leaning Tower of Pisa.

4 Al Maqtaa Fort

V4 Al Maqtaa Bridge

This small 200-year-old fort once guarded the main approach to the city and still stands sentinel beside Al Maqtaa Bridge. Its sand-coloured exterior is adorned with carved wooden doors and shuttered windows, with narrow slits above for rifles.

7 Bain al Jessrain (Between the Bridges)
ABU DHABI-AL AIN RD
AL MAQTA
Abu Dhabi Creek
KHOR AL MAQTA'A
Souk Qaryat al Beri
Shangri-La Hotel
0 metres 800
0 yards 800
AL KHALEEJ AL ARABI ST
Yas Island
Zeraa Island
E10
E12
Yas Hotel
Yas Marina
YAS PLAZA
Abu Dhabi International
MASDAR CITY
MADINAT KHALIFA
AIRPORT RD
E20

1 Top 10 Sights p99
1 Places to Eat p103
1 Bars p102

5 Aldar HQ

W4 Al Raha, next to the Dubai–Abu Dhabi Hwy

The Aldar HQ is another strong contender for the title of Abu Dhabi's most unusual building. It is clearly visible from the main highway as you approach from Dubai. Claimed to be the world's first circular skyscraper, the structure looks a lot like a huge magnifying glass, supported by a diagonal grid of steel girders. It is also one of Abu Dhabi's first eco-friendly buildings, constructed using recyclable materials like steel, concrete and glass. Visitors are welcome to step inside and explore the spacious atrium.

6 Manarat Al Saadiyat

V2 Sheikh Khalifa Hwy 9am–8pm daily manaratalsaadiyat.ae

Located in the Saadiyat Cultural District, Manarat Al Saadiyat is a vibrant arts and cultural hub. It hosts a range of events, including art exhibitions, workshops, talks and performances, fostering creativity and dialogue. The venue is also home to the annual Abu Dhabi Art Fair that showcases contemporary international artists, reinforcing the UAE's position in the international art world. Free guided tours can be booked by writing to manaratalsaadiyat@dctabudhabi.ae.

7 Bain al Jessrain

V4 Souk Qaryat al Beri: 10am–10pm daily (from 4pm Fri) soukqaryatalberi.com

Most of Abu Dhabi is actually built on an island separated from the mainland by a narrow sea inlet known as Maqta Creek – it wasn't until the opening of Maqta Bridge in 1966 that the island and mainland were connected. Three bridges span the creek, whose shores feature several top hotels and some of the city's most valuable real estate. The area on the mainland side, known as Bain al Jessrain (Between the Bridges), is also where you'll find the little Souk Qaryat al Beri, which houses a string of multiple boutique and eating outlets set over two levels. Following a Venetian theme, canals meander throughout the pretty souk.

8 Mangrove National Park

U3 Eastern Ring Rd 10am–midnight daily ead.gov.ae

Home to nearly 75 per cent of the UAE's total mangrove forest coverage, the Mangrove National Park is a green haven nestled away from the hustle and bustle of Abu Dhabi. Visitors can

Relaxing on the white sands of Saadiyat Public Beach

explore the park through kayak tours or use binoculars to spot over 60 bird species that thrive within the park.

9 Louvre Abu Dhabi

V2 Saadiyat Cultural District, Saadiyat Island 10am–6:30pm Tue–Thu, 10am–8:30pm Fri–Sun louvreabudhabi.ae

A branch of the famous Parisian museum, and one of the largest art museums in the Arabian Peninsula, this is the centrepiece of the Saadiyat Cultural District. The building resembles a seemingly weightless, enormous silvery flying saucer under an intricately latticed roof that allows light to enter through perforations. The museum hosts rotating exhibits from the Louvre's collections, including a strong selection of Middle Eastern and Islamic art, and also organizes film screenings.

10 Saadiyat Public Beach

V2 8am–sunset daily

This beautiful beach offers a nice change of pace from the city centre, with a huge expanse of fine white sand. The dunes behind the beach are a nesting site for turtles and a refuge for other rare flora and fauna. You might even spot dolphins offshore here. The beach is equipped with facilities, including toilets, showers and a café.

A DAY AROUND ABU DHABI

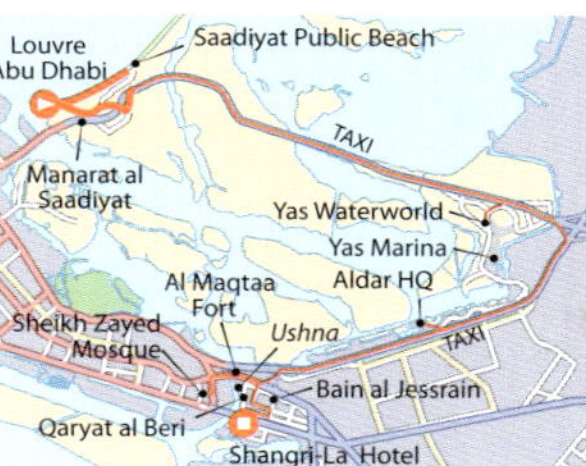

Morning

Start by exploring the myriad treasures of the **Louvre Abu Dhabi**, including a large selection of Middle Eastern and Islamic art. Afterwards, pop into the nearby **Manarat al Saadiyat** exhibition to see what the future of Abu Dhabi looks like. If museums aren't your thing, spend some time on the **Saadiyat Public Beach** or brave the looping rides and slides of **Yas Waterworld** *(p48)*. Pick up some lunch either in the museum or at one of the many places to eat in the **Yas Marina** *(p36)*.

Afternoon

Head back to the mainland. If you have time, see the innovative **Aldar HQ** building en route. Spend the rest of the afternoon at the iconic **Sheikh Zayed Mosque** *(p36)* and admire its ornate courtyard and interior.

Close to evening, catch a cab to **Bain al Jessrain**. Look out for the 200-year-old **Al Maqtaa Fort** *(p99)* and then explore the boutiques and restaurants in **Qaryat al Beri** souk. Watch the sun set over the historic Maqtaa Creek with a cocktail at the kitsch **Ushna** *(p103)*. Afterwards, head to one of the excellent restaurants here. **Bord Eau** *(p103)* at the Shangri-La Hotel is a lovely place for a romantic evening meal, with sweeping creek views from the terrace.

Brick-vaulted ceiling and chic seating area at Y Bar

Bars

1. Y Bar

W4 Yas Island Rotana Hotel Noon–2am daily rotana.com

A funky bar with an outdoor terrace. It's a great place for evening cocktails.

2. Cabana 9, Saadiyat Beach Club

V2 Saadiyat Island 10am–sunset daily saadiyatbeach club.ae

Sip a drink overlooking the sea at this idyllic beachfront pool bar.

3. Relax@12

V3 Aloft Hotel, Khaleej al Arabi St 5pm till late daily relaxat12abudhabi.com

A cool rooftop bar with sweeping views. Visiting DJs keep things lively.

4. Buddha-Bar Beach Abu Dhabi

V2 The St. Regis Saadiyat Island Resort Hours vary, check website buddhabar beachabudhabi.com

A legendary pub providing a beach-themed experience in Abu Dhabi with tropical interiors and creative cocktails.

5. Poolside

V4 Fairmont Bab Al Bahr, Khor Al Maqta 9am–6pm daily fairmont.com

This pool bar is the best place to soak up creek views and sip tasty cocktails, alongside gourmet burgers.

6. Stars 'N' Bars

W4 Yas Island, Abu Dhabi 11:30–2am daily abudhabi. starsnbars.ae

Enjoy varied international cuisine along with free arcade games at this American-style sports bar.

7. Sorso

V4 The Ritz-Carlton Abu Dhabi, Grand Canal 5pm–1am daily ritzcarlton.com

A smart bar that looks like the lounge of an old-school European gentlemen's club, with huge arm-chairs and plush sofas.

8. Belgian Café

W4 Radisson Blu Hotel, Yas Island Noon–2am daily (to 3am Thu & Fri) radissonhotels.com

A chic café serving lunch and dinner favourites accompanied by a fine selection of Belgian beverages.

9. Iris Yas Island

W4 Yas Yacht Club, Yas Marina 6pm–3am Mon–Sat yasmarina.ae

Pose with a drink at this chic bar-club, while admiring views of Yas Marina.

10. Wet Deck

W4 W Abu Dhabi, Yas Island May–Sep: 8pm–2am daily; Oct–Apr: 6pm–1am daily marriott.com

A hip venue set under a dramatic latticed roof, with a nightly DJ.

Places to Eat

PRICE CATEGORIES

For a three-course meal for one with half a bottle of wine (or equivalent meal), taxes and extra charges.

D under AED 100 **DD** AED 100–400 **DDD** over AED 400

1. Bord Eau

V4 Shangri-La Hotel, Qaryat al Beri 6:30–11:30pm daily shangri-la.com • DDD

This elegant restaurant offers classic French dishes and modern cuisine. There is also a really excellent wine list.

2. Sardinia

U3 Abu Dhabi Country Club 3pm–midnight daily adcountry club.com • DD

An award-winning kitchen serving international cuisine. Complimentary *amuse-bouche* is served between each course.

3. Entrecôte Café de Paris

V4 Shangri-La Hotel, Qaryat al Beri Noon–midnight daily entrecote.me • DD

This branch of the famous Geneva restaurant serves a single dish – the famed entrecôte fillet steak, in a secret sauce.

4. Pappas Taverna

W4 W Abu Dhabi, Yas Island 7pm–11pm Wed–Mon (from 2pm Fri) marriott.com • DD

Sample creative Mediterranean dishes in a setting inspired by Greece's coastline.

5. Shang Palace

V4 Shangri-La Hotel, Qaryat al Beri Noon–3pm & 7–11:30pm daily shangri-la.com • DD

Enjoy excellent Chinese cuisine cooked with panache by top-tier chefs.

Elegantly designed interior of the Sofra Bld

6. Daikan Izakaya

W4 Yas Bay, Yas Island 5pm–1am daily daikan.ae • DD

Enjoy a traditional *izakaya* experience at this relaxed Japanese spot, which specializes in ramen and expertly grilled *yakitori*.

7. Brooklyn Chop House

W4 W Abu Dhabi, Yas Island Hours vary, check website marriott.com • DD

Known for its Asian flavours, this New York-style steakhouse serves premium steaks alongside dim sum and Peking duck.

8. Cipriani

W4 Marina Mall 6pm–midnight daily cipriani.com• DD

Sample an à la carte menu of Venetian and Italian cuisine prepared with seasonal ingredients.

9. Ushna

V4 Souk Qaryat al Beri 12:30–11pm daily ushna.ae • DD

A chic North Indian restaurant in an attractive waterside setting.

10. Sofra Bld

V4 Shangri-La Hotel, Qaryat al Beri 6–11pm daily shangri-la.com • DD

Traditional Arabian and Asian cuisines are prepared at several chef stations, offering diners the opportunity to interact with the chefs as they create the delicious dishes.

STREETSMART

A metro train in Dubai

GETTING AROUND

Whether exploring Dubai and Abu Dhabi by foot or making use of public transport, here is everything you need to know to navigate the two cities and the areas beyond like a pro.

AT A GLANCE

PUBLIC TRANSPORT COSTS

NOL RED TICKET

AED 4.00

For a trip in Dubai within one zone.

NOL 1-DAY GOLD PASS

AED 20

For one day's unlimited travel.

ABU DHABI BUS

AED 2.00

For a single bus trip in Abu Dhabi.

SPEED LIMITS

URBAN SINGLE LANE ROAD

40-60 km/h (25-38 mph)

URBAN DUAL CARRIAGEWAY

80 km/h (50 mph)

DUBAI FREEWAY

120 km/h (75 mph)

ABU DHABI-AL AIN HIGHWAY

160 km/h (100 mph)

Arriving by Air

Located just outside the old city, **Dubai Airport** is one of the world's best. Emirates airline has its own terminal (3), while most other long-haul international flights land at Terminal 1.

Abu Dhabi Airport is also modern in design and international visitors will arrive into the circular terminal (1).

There are taxis at both airports. In Dubai there are fixed rates from the airport to various parts of the city. Terminals 1 and 3 are both connected to the Dubai Metro and there are various airport buses, including the **Sky Bus** *(Terhab)*, which runs 24 hours from all terminals. To get from Abu Dhabi airport to the city, you'll have to catch a taxi or ride the 24-hour airport bus #A1.

Abu Dhabi Airport
W abudhabiairport.ae
Dubai Airport
W dubaiairports.ae
Sky Bus
W dubai-buses.com

Arriving by Road

It is possible to drive to the UAE and there are five border crossings available from Oman. However the UAE's borders with Saudi Arabia are open only to Gulf Corporation Council (GCC) nationals.

Arriving by Sea

Many cruise ships include Dubai in their trips, docking at **Dubai Cruise Terminal** in Port Rashid, or the **Dubai Harbour Cruise Terminal** in Dubai Marina.

Dubai Cruise Terminal
W dubaicruiseterminal.com
Dubai Harbour Cruise Terminal
W cruisedubai.com

Tickets

All public transport on land in Dubai is controlled by **RTA** and is covered by the **Nol** ticketing system. Buy tickets before travelling; none are sold on board any form of transport. The cheapest option is the reusable Nol Red Ticket. To use this you need to pre-pay the correct fare for each journey you make. You can also buy a one-day travel pass, offering unlimited transport. There are three types of rechargeable Nol cards (Silver, Gold and Blue) which can be pre-loaded with up to AED 500 of credit. Cards/tickets can be bought and topped up at any metro station.

Nol
W rta.ae
RTA
W rta.ae

Travelling by Metro

The driverless Dubai Metro is by far the quickest and cheapest way to get around. There are two lines, Red and Green, which cover the city's seven transport zones and most of the sights. Trains run daily from around 5:30am to midnight (later on Thursday) and from 10am on Friday. There are departures every five to ten minutes. Children under five or shorter than 0.9m travel free.

Travelling by Tram

The **Dubai Tram** loops around the marina and continues up the coast for several kilometres, providing access to places the metro doesn't reach. The system connects to the metro and also links to the Palm Monorail *(p89)*.

Dubai Tram
W alsufouhtram.com

Travelling by Bus

Dubai Buses has an extensive bus network, although services tend to cover less-visited areas. Abu Dhabi buses **(DoT)** are more useful, with routes criss-crossing Downtown. Fares are around AED 3–4 per journey. There are also bus services between the two cities.

DoT
W dot.abudhabi.ae

Travelling by Car

Driving in the UAE can be challenging, given the regular heavy traffic, labyrinthine road layouts and often aggressive driving styles, but is feasible if you're confident behind the wheel. Cars drive on the right. Drinking and driving is a punishable offence and receives severe penalties. There are car-hire desks at airports, hotels and other locations. The international car-hire companies **Avis** and **Europcar** are well represented.

Avis
W avis.com
Europcar
W europcardubai.com
W europcar-abudhabi.com

Travelling by Taxi

Taxis in both Dubai and Abu Dhabi can be hailed anywhere on the street, and there are taxi ranks at most shopping malls – during busy times it's better to call ahead. All taxis use meters and cost around AED 1.5 per km plus starting fare. In Dubai, the this fare is AED 5, with a minimum charge of AED 12. In Abu Dhabi, the starting fare is AED 3.50 (AED 4 at night; minimum fare AED 10 from 10pm to 6am). Reputable companies are the **Dubai Taxi Corporation** and **TransAD** (for Abu Dhabi).

Dubai Taxi Corporation
W dubaitaxi.ae
TransAD
W transad.ae

Travelling by Boat

The plush **Dubai Ferry** runs three times daily between Bur Dubai and Dubai Marina (75 minutes), and there are also various sightseeing round trips. Fares on all trips are AED 50. In the old city, *abras* criss-cross Dubai Creek. The fare is AED 1 per person.

Dubai Ferry
W dubai-ferry.com

Cycling

In both Dubai and Abu Dhabi, bikes can be hired through **Byky**. Cycling infrastructure is improving in Dubai, with camel tracks at Nad Al Sheba converted into cycle lanes and the Al Qudra Cycle Track stretching out into the desert.

Byky
W q8byky.com

PRACTICAL INFORMATION

A little local know-how goes a long way in Dubai and Abu Dhabi. On these pages, you can find all the essential advice and information you will need to make the most of your trip to these cities.

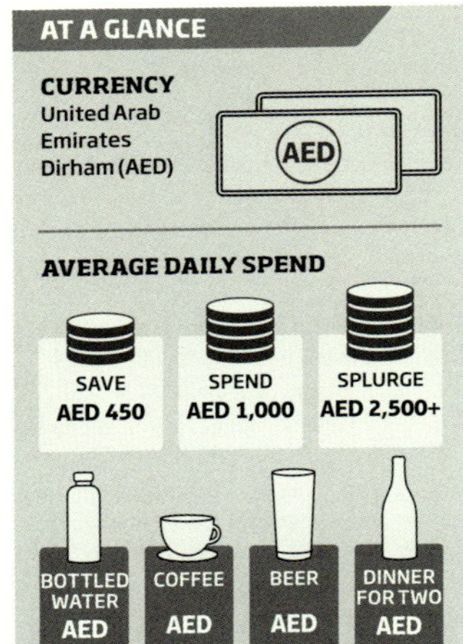

ESSENTIAL PHRASES

Hello	marhaba
Goodbye	maasalaamah
Please	min fadlik/ min fadlak
Thank you	shukran
I don't understand...	la'afham

ELECTRICITY SUPPLY

Standard voltage is 220/240 voltes. Power sockets fit the three-prong type G plug used in the UK, but you may also see type C plugs.

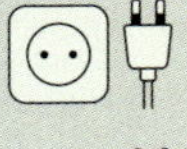

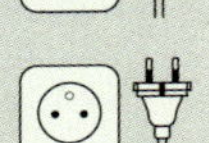

Passports and Visas

For entry requirements, including visas, consult your nearest United Arab Emirates embassy or check the **General Directorate of Residency and Foreigners Affairs** website. Free 30-day or 90-day visit visas are available on arrival for some countries. Visas for 30 days (but not for 90 days) can be extended by the **General Directorate**. Passports must be valid for six months from the date of entry to the UAE.

Canada, the UK, the US and other countries have consular representation in the region.

General Directorate of Residency and Foreigners Affairs
W gdrfad.gov.ae

Government Advice

Now more than ever, it is important to consult both your and the UAE government's advice before travelling. The UK Foreign, Commonwealth and Development Office **(FCDO)**, the **US Department of State**, the **Australian Department of Foreign Affairs and Trade** and the **UAE Government Portal** offer the latest information on security, health and local regulations.

Australian Department of Foreign Affairs and Trade
W smartraveller.gov.au

FCDO
W gov.uk/foreign-traveladvice

UAE Government Portal
W u.ae/en

US Department of State
W travel.state.gov

Customs Information

You can find information on the laws relating to goods and currency taken in or out of the UAE on the **Dubai Customs** website. The duty-free allowance for each traveller is 400 cigarettes, 500g (18 oz) of tobacco, 50 cigars and 4 litres of alcohol. Alcohol cannot be bought from local shops without a liquor licence (only available to UAE residents), so buy duty free at the airport if you want to have your own supply at home.

In addition to the usual items (firearms, illegal drugs and pornography), it is forbidden to bring in any banned movies, TV programmes and offensive publications, especially films and programmes that include scenes with passionate kissing, sex, nudity or semi-nudity, or drug use. Goods made in Israel (or bearing Israeli logos) are also forbidden.

Dubai Customs
W dubaicustoms.gov.ae

Insurance

We recommend that you take out a comprehensive insurance policy covering theft, loss of belongings, medical care, cancellations and delays, and read the small print carefully.

If you plan to go scuba diving you may need additional coverage.

Vaccinations

No inoculations are required for visiting the UAE.

Money

The UAE's currency is the United Arab Emirates dirham, written as AED or Dh. One dirham is divided into 100 fils. Currency notes are in denominations of AED 5, AED 10, AED 20, AED 50, AED 100, AED 200, AED 500 and AED 1,000, while coins are in amounts such as 25 fils, 50 fils and one dirham. The UAE dirham is pegged to the US dollar. US$1 is equal to AED 3.67. All other currencies fluctuate and should be checked before you travel.

There are branches of numerous international banks in the UAE, such as HSBC, Citibank and Standard Chartered Bank. Alongside these, good local banks include National Bank of Abu Dhabi, Mashreq Bank and Emirates National Bank of Dubai. Globally linked ATMs are located everywhere in both cities. American Express, Mastercard and Visa are widely accepted, and credit cards and contactless payments can be used almost anywhere. If you intend to shop in the souks or other parts of the old towns, it's advisable to carry a small amount of cash as there may be additional fees for using cards. There are also several bureaux de change, such as the leading **Al Ansari Exchange**, which has branches all over the city, including in many malls. Bringing cash from home and changing it locally is often cheaper than using cards, which can mean having to pay hefty credit card and ATM fees.

Although tipping is not common or expected, it is always appreciated.

Al Ansari Exchange
W alansariexchange.com

Opening Hours

Business hours in the UAE aren't fixed but, generally, shopping malls and supermarkets are open daily 10am–10pm (sometimes later at weekends). Shops in the streets open at approximately the same times but often close for lunch from 1 to 4 or 5pm. The UAE weekend is Friday and Saturday and hours may change on these days.

Opening hours for museums and attractions can fluctuate wildly and some places close during the afternoon. Many restaurants have regular happy hours (generally 6–8pm daily).

The holy month of Ramadan presents some challenges to visitors. Although you are not expected to join the fasting, you should be tolerant of those who are practising their faith. Laws for food establishments during Ramadan have become more relaxed since 2018 and bars and restaurants generally remain open as usual, particularly in the more popular tourist areas.

Situations can change quickly and unexpectedly. Always check before visiting attractions and hospitality venues for up-to-date opening hours and booking requirements.

Travellers with Specific Requirements

Developers have worked hard to cater to visitors with specific requirements in many of Dubai and Abu Dhabi's newest hotels and resorts. Infrastructure in the cities is generally wheelchair accessible, including most buses and trains. Most of the more modern and upmarket hotels now have specially adapted rooms, although this can be harder to find in cheaper accommodation and in the old parts of both cities. Do not expect to find much infrastructure for those with specific requirements in the rural desert areas outside of the both cities.

There are excellent transport services at both airports for visitors with disabilities, while the Dubai Metro contains tactile guide paths, wheelchair spaces in compartments and other facilities. The **Visit Dubai** website has a number of pages dedicated to accessible travel, and can direct you to helpful resources, both online and on the ground, when visiting the UAE.

Visit Dubai
W visitdubai.com

Language

The official language of the United Arab Emirates is Arabic, with Modern Standard Arabic taught in schools. The majority of locally born Emiratis speak a Gulf Arabic dialect that is broadly similar to that spoken in other countries in the region.
A broad array of languages are spoken among the large and diverse expatriate community, including dialects of Pashto, Hindi, Balochi and Persian. English is the most widely spoken language in Dubai, and is also generally spoken and understood across Abu Dhabi.

Personal Security

Dubai and Abu Dhabi are both safe places for most visitors and petty crime is almost unheard of. It is still advisable to be sensible and avoid leaving valuables unattended. When visiting popular historical areas, particularly around the souks in the old part of Dubai, avoid the numerous touts who attempt to sell "copy watches" or "copy bags" and so on. These industries can be highly unethical. If you do lose anything, contact the Police Lost and

AT A GLANCE

EMERGENCY NUMBERS

POLICE	AMBULANCE	FIRE DEPARTMENT
999	998	997

TIME ZONE

The UAE time zone is GMT+4. There is no daylight saving time.

TAP WATER

Tap water is safe to drink across the UAE, but some places may suggest bottled water due to piping issues..

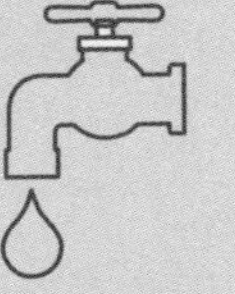

WEBSITES AND APPS

Visit Dubai
The website of Dubai's tourist board *(visitdubai.com)* provides information on local events and also has an app.

Visit Abu Dhabi
The website and app for tourism in Abu Dhabi *(visitabudhabi.ae)*.

Careem
This ride-hailing app has options for all budgets, from taxis to high-end transport.

Eco Tourism UAE
An app with information and advice on eco-friendly travel in the UAE.

Found. If you leave something behind in a taxi in Dubai, you'll need to file a report at Dubai Taxi *(p107)*. If your taxi driver is driving too fast or recklessly, tell them to slow down *(shway shway)*.

If you're driving and you have an accident, first get out of harm's way, then call the police for instructions. Decelerate or pull over in sand storms when visibility is poor. Note also that drivers generally will not stop for pedestrians on a crossing, so cross only at lights where possible.

Although people of all races and religions are welcome, the UAE is an Islamic state and it is advisable to exercise caution as you can land in trouble for not respecting local religious customs and decency laws. Arrests have resulted from foreigners being too affectionate in public. If you are arrested, do not immediately sign anything in Arabic if instructed to. Your consulate should be your first call – they can help facilitate contact with a local bilingual lawyer.

Homosexuality is illegal in the UAE and punishable with harsh penalties, although these are very rarely enforced. Though both Dubai and Abu Dhabi have large expat communities who may be more accepting of all people, it is still important to keep in mind state law and to act accordingly. Male visitors may also be solicited by sex workers in local bars, especially in the older parts of the cities later in the evenings.

Women travelling solo in the UAE shouldn't experience any harassment if they follow local norms but should still take normal precautions. Sit in the back seat of taxis and in the "women's section" of buses. Dedicated women's queues at banks and government departments indicate that women will get preferential service.

When swimming, take any warning signs regarding dangerous rips and strong undertows seriously. In spite of the calm appearance of the water around the city, Dubai's beaches tend to have very powerful undercurrents.

Health

The UAE has a world-class healthcare system, with highly efficient hospitals, but services are expensive. Full health insurance *(p109)*, arranged before your trip, is advised.

Standards are outstanding in both private and public hospitals, although the services are generally faster at the emergency departments in private hospitals. Good hospitals for tourists include the **American Hospital** and **Emirates Hospital** in Dubai, and the **Burjeel Hospital** and **Cleveland Clinic** in Abu Dhabi.

There are numerous pharmacies within both cities that can offer advice on minor ailments. Many are open 24 hours a day (ask at your hotel for the nearest branch).

American Hospital
W ahdubai.com
Burjeel Hospital
W burjeel.com
Cleveland Clinic
W clevelandclinicabudhabi.ae
Emirates Hospital
W emirateshospital.ae

Smoking, Alcohol and Drugs

Smoking is prohibited in bars, restaurants, clubs and cafés in the UAE. It is also forbidden to smoke on public transport. Some of these places and means of transport may have designated smoking areas, but check the rules in these places, which should be closely obeyed. You will see many bars offering sheesha, which is legal for users over the age of 18.

Generally, the legal drinking age in Abu Dhabi is 18, but a by-law prevents hotels from serving alcohol to those under the age of 21. In Dubai the drinking age is 21. It is prohibited to drive under the influence of alcohol or other substances; those caught doing so will at least fined and may lose their driving licence *(p107)*.

Penalties for the use and trafficking of drugs are severe, with fines and sentences often imposed.

ID

You will need photo ID when buying alcohol, and often for entry into bars and nightclubs. It is not a legal requirement to carry picture ID at all times but a valid driving licence will be required if you want to hire a car.

Responsible Travel

The UAE has one of the largest ecological footprints in the world, but the government is working to enhance its sustainable practices. The Dubai Department of Tourism and Commerce Marketing have a "Green Tourism Award" programme and many travel providers have taken steps to lessen the carbon footprint of the services they offer.

Given the desert location of the UAE, there is a water scarcity here. Do your bit by avoiding long showers and reusing towels. Additionally, avoid single-use plastic water bottles through carrying a reusable metal bottle. Look for hotels with the Dubai Sustainable Tourism Stamp, which recognizes places for their high levels of sustainability.

When out and about, travellers are advised to seek out activities with lower emissions. A whole host of activities are available, including hiking and camping in the Hajar Mountains, scuba-diving and snorkelling outings on the UAE's coast, or bird-watching adventures. Be sure to use reef-safe sunscreen when swimming or diving to minimize your impact on the marine environment.

For more information, consult the UAE government's website.

Mobile Phones and Wi-Fi

To phone a mobile in the UAE from abroad, dial the UAE country code 971 followed by 50, 55 or 56 and the mobile number. Within the UAE, dial 050, 055 or 056 for mobiles, adding 04 to call Dubai from outside the emirate and 02 to call Abu Dhabi from another emirate.

If you need a mobile, it's generally easier (and cheaper) to get a local SIM card. The national telecommunications company **Etisalat** offers visitors a useful "Visitor Mobile Line", which gives you a SIM card and allows you to make calls at local rates. The card is available at the Etisalat shops and other outlets. You will need to present your passport when purchasing a SIM card.

There is Wi-Fi access everywhere. Etisalat operates numerous Wi-Fi "hotspots" in shopping malls, restaurants, coffee shops and elsewhere. You can pay online with a credit card, with rates starting at around AED 15 per hour.

Etisalat
W aramex.com

Postal Services

Emirates Post is the UAE's national postal service. You can buy stamps at any post office and at some stationery shops. Mail to Europe, North America and Australasia takes about 10 days. It is unreliable, however, so register anything valuable or use a courier for anything urgent. Companies with a good reputation for service include **Aramex** and **FedEx**. All will pick up from your hotel. You can pay on collection if you don't have an account.

Aramex
W aramex.com
Emirates Post
W emiratespost.com
FedEx
W fedex.com/ae

Taxes and Refunds

The standard VAT rate in the UAE is 5 per cent on all taxable supplies and imports. Tourists and visitors are eligible for refunds on VAT paid on purchases they made during their stay.

Trips and Tours

There are dozens of tour operators in both Dubai and Abu Dhabi offering a varied range of desert outings, trips to neighbouring cities and emirates, and dinner *dhow* cruises.

A number of organizations offer desert safaris. Before you book, ensure you check the sustainability and animal welfare credentials. **Arabian Adventures** *(p40)* is the biggest and best, with a variety of sustainably run tours, led by professionally trained guides with full knowledge of desert flora and fauna.

In both Dubai and Abu Dhabi, there are hop-on hop-off sightseeing bus tours run by **Big Bus Tours**. *Abras*, or water taxis, can be chartered for private cruises up and down the creek in Dubai. They also run frequently along other main routes, towards two stations in Deira and two in Bur Dubai. Visit the **Dubai Online** website for timetables and more information. There are also sightseeing trips aboard the **Dubai Ferry**.

Walking tours of Al Fahidi are offered by the SMCCU *(p69)*, and interesting foodie tours of offbeat Dubai eateries by **Frying Pan Adventures**. For a walk on the wild side in the mountains of the UAE, contact **Absolute Adventure** or **UAE Trekkers**.

Absolute Adventure
W adventure.ae
Big Bus Tours
W bigbustours.com
Dubai Ferry
W dubai-ferry.com
Dubai Online
W dubai-online.com/transport/abra
Frying Pan Adventures
W fryingpanadventures.com
UAE Trekkers
W uaetrekkers.com

Shopping

There are two types of shopping in Dubai and Abu Dhabi: modern malls and traditional souks. Shopping malls are found everywhere, from huge mega-developments to low-key local places. Many leading local and international shops have outlets in malls, and chains such as Damas (jewellery), Paris Gallery (perfume) and Grand Stores (electronics) can be found in almost all the major shopping centres. Prices are fixed and cards are generally accepted.

Shopping in traditional souks in the old city is a different affair. Prices are generally lower and haggling is expected (credit cards may not be accepted except for big-ticket items so check before you buy). A lot of the items on sale consist of everyday essentials, but you'll also find some interesting products such as gold, spices, perfumes, designer fakes and antiques. Shops in Karama Souk *(p72)* have a vast array of well-priced and convincing fakes.

Dining

There's a huge range of places to eat in both Dubai and Abu Dhabi, from inexpensive local cafés to extravagant fine-dining venues overseen by some of the best Michelin-starred chefs.

Beyond this, there's also a huge array of cuisines on offer in both cities. This is one of the best places to sample classic dishes from across the Middle East, including traditional Arabian cuisine (or "Lebanese", as it is often described), along with Iranian, Moroccan and Emirati specialities. Indian, Italian and Chinese cuisine is also popular.

Cheaper places are aimed largely at expats from across Asia who live in the city, hence the many Indian and Pakistani restaurants across the old city. Plenty of cafés serve a range of Arabian food, including shawarma kebabs in pitta bread.

More expensive places are largely attached to hotels and come in every possible shape and form, from opulent Arabian-themed venues to chic bolt holes. Dining next to the sea is popular, and many places offer outdoor terraces – those with outdoor seating may also offer sheesha (waterpipes). Happy hours (typically from 6pm to 8pm) can make drinks much cheaper.

A 10 per cent service charge may be added to cover the tip, along with other taxes. These can add up to 25 per cent of the basic cost of a meal and drinks, so check whether they're included before you order.

Children are well catered for, except at the very best fine-dining restaurants.

PLACES TO STAY

Dubai and Abu Dhabi are the land of luxury. Top stays are more grand, more luxurious and better equipped than almost anywhere else. That said, there are still affordable options and an increasing number of fun and fashionable mid-range options to suit all budgets.

Summer is the most affordable time to visit, when temperatures rise above 40 degrees. Conversely, prices spike during the cooler months, particularly around Christmas and the New Year. Across the UAE, the tourism tax is between AED 7 and AED 20 per night.

PRICE CATEGORIES

For a standard double room per night (with breakfast if included), taxes and extra charges.

D under AED 600
DD AED 600–1,500
DDD over AED 1,500

Deira

Park Hyatt Dubai

E2 Dubai Creek Golf & Yacht Club hyatt.com · DDD

If you want to experience a life of serenity, look no further than the Park Hyatt. This hotel has a private adults-only infinity lagoon on the shores of Dubai Creek, making it easy to forget about the outside world while luxuriating in a private cabana. Kids are well catered for too with a splash pool for little ones and a great kids' club for older ones.

Aloft Dubai Creek

E2 Baniyas Road marriott.com · D

Few budget-friendly hotels are better located than Aloft Dubai Creek. It's right next to the creek, with its many sights and souks, and has an entry to Deira City Centre mall, allowing you to shop like a local all day long. After spending time exploring, retreat to the rooftop infinity pool to enjoy the sweeping views of Deira.

Sheraton Dubai Creek Hotel & Towers

E2 Baniyas Road marriott.com · DD

This long-standing hotel overlooks the historical Dubai Creek and even has 30 luxury suites perched directly above the creek. While the location is excellent, the food is the main draw. From Vivaldi, a top Italian restaurant, to the Chelsea Arms, Dubai's oldest British pub, you can't go wrong with hotel dining here.

Bur Dubai

XVA Art Hotel

K2 Al Fahidi Historical District xvahotel.com · DD

Step back in time at this heritage boutique in the oldest inhabited part of Dubai. The hotel has a suitably old-world feel, which is enhanced by the classical Emirati features, including three wind towers and two interior courtyards. You'll also find eclectic art on all the walls and a packed schedule of events, which means there is plenty to do beyond admiring the old architecture.

Al Seef Heritage Hotel Dubai, Curio Collection by Hilton

K2 Al Seef, Dubai Creek jumeirah.com · D

This spot is a one-of-a-kind "street" hotel, spread throughout the Al Seef Historical District. Unlike other places, the hotel eschews the modern look, instead using the historical buildings and their traditional Bedouin interiors, filled with stone-plastered walls and wood ceilings. Despite being spread across Al Seef, the hotel makes getting around easy, thanks to its fleet of golf carts.

Downtown Dubai

Armani Hotel Dubai

C6 Burj Khalifa armanihoteldubai.com · DDD

Spread across 11 floors of the world's tallest building, the Burj Khalifa *(p22)*, is this hotel that's devoted to style. The interiors are informed by the impeccable taste of designer Giorgio Armani. The result is a luxurious mix of Arabian and Italian design. The hotel also has direct access to the Dubai Mall, so you can create your own style.

The Lana – Dorchester Collection

C7 Marasi Drive, Business Bay dorchestercollection.com · DDD

The Lana has everything you might need for the ultimate pampering stay. Beyond the 225 ultra-luxurious rooms and suites, this canal-side gem is home to the region's first Dior spa with an array of unique treatments. Afterwards, head up to the rooftop pool for incredible views of the Burj Khalifa before dinner at acclaimed chef Martín Berasategui's first restaurant outside of Spain.

25hours Hotel One Central

E6 Trade Centre Street 25hours-hotels.com · DD

This mid-range Dubai hotel embodies the ethos of work hard, play hard. During the day, the fun, creatively designed co-working spaces serve as tranquil places to get work done. But in the evening, there are five restaurants, on-site bike rentals and a cinema to fill the hours. Check in to experience the perfect of work-life balance.

Mama Shelter Dubai

B7 Business Bay mamashelter.com · DD

At Mama Shelter, the only rule is to have fun – and the hotel offers plenty of ways to do this. There's the rooftop pool, shaded with colourful canopies, to splash around in, the outdoor CineMama that shows classic movies and big sports matches, and the range of daily events. Be sure to finish your day at the terrace restaurant where you can sample delicious homemade Middle Eastern fare.

Rove Downtown

D6 Near Dubai Mall rovehotels.com · D

Rove is a rare budget-friendly spot in Downtown. But don't think the lower price means there is a lack of amenities. Beyond the more than 400 well-equipped rooms, Rove has a lovely outdoor pool, a 24-hour gym and a co-working space, ideal for business people and digital nomads.

Jumeirah

Jumeirah Al Naseem

C1 Madinat Jumeirah jumeirah.com · DDD

You'll never be bored at this luxury five-star hotel. It's located in a complex with a water park, tennis courts, fitness centre and luxury spa. Within the hotel grounds there are 11 bars and restaurants as well as five pools, with specific areas designated for both kids and adults. You'll feel all the better knowing there's an on-site rehabilitation lagoon for injured Gulf turtles.

Jumeirah Marsa Al Arab

C1 Jumeirah Beach Road jumeirah.com · DDD

Want to soak up as much of the Dubai sunshine as possible? Look no further than Jumeirah Marsa Al Arab. Every room in this ultra-luxury resort comes with its own sun-drenched terrace. Add in its private beach, four pools and a superyacht-filled marina, and there's plenty of opportunity to while away your hours outdoors. When night falls, head to one of the 11 restaurants for a top-tier dining experience.

Jumeirah Burj Al Arab

C1 Jumeirah Beach Road jumeirah.com · DDD

Within the iconic sail-shaped Burj Al Arab *(p30)* is the unofficial "seven-star hotel", one that takes extravagant luxury to a whole new level. All rooms include a private butler as well as clocks by Rolex, bedspreads from Versace and toiletries by Hermés. Guests can move around town with the Rolls Royce chauffeur service and depart in style from the rooftop helipad. What more could you need?

Mandarin Oriental Jumeira, Dubai

C4 Jumeirah Beach Road mandarinoriental.com · DDD

This resort hotel has excellent views no matter which way you look – the glittering Gulf sea on one side and the glitzy lights of Dubai's skyline on the other. It's a good thing then that each room comes with a balcony to soak up the views (there's no bad option). Enjoy both views with excellent Portuguese cuisine at the rooftop restaurant Tasca, by renowned chef José Avillez.

Kempinski Hotel Mall of the Emirates

C2 Sheikh Zayed Road kempinski.com · DDD

As the name suggests, this hotel is attached to the Mall of the Emirates, and is ideal for shopaholics. But there's more to the Kempinski than just shopping. Step inside to discover a winter wonderland with ski chalet-style suites overlooking the mall's snow park, Ski Dubai. It feels like Christmas all year round – until you step outside.

Rove La Mer Beach

D4 La Mer rovehotels.com · D

If you want to spend your time relaxing by water, this branch of the budget-friendly Rove chain is for you. The hotel has a prime beachfront location, with cool waters perfect for cooling off during the sweltering days. If you don't want to leave the hotel grounds, there's also a large outdoor pool to lounge by or swim in.

Dubai Marina and Palm Jumeirah

One&Only The Palm

B1 Palm Jumeirah oneandonlyresorts.com · DDD

A stay at the One&Only is an exercise in treating yourself. Whether it's a meal at the Michelin-starred STAY, run by chef Yannick Alléno, or a treatment at the French-Arabian fusion Guerlain Spa, your stay here is guaranteed to be a pampered experience.

Banyan Tree Dubai

B1 Bluewaters Island banyantree.com · DDD

Seeking a restorative retreat? Look no further than Banyan Tree Dubai. The staff at the wellness centre will work with you to compile a personalized health programme, tailored to what you need from your break. Facilities include a gym, vitality pools and even a restaurant-inspired spa. This is true bliss.

Atlantis, The Royal

B1 Palm Jumeirah atlantis.com · DDD

This opulent hotel, one of the top 10 hotels in the world, defines luxury. The rooms, suites and signature penthouses are all outfitted in grand style: think gold bookcases, floor-to-ceiling windows and opulent pink-marble bathrooms. The dining options are equally top-tier, with the first daytime Nobu restaurant right on the beach, and culinary options that traverse the globe, from Peru to Iran.

Atlantis, The Palm

B1 Palm Jumeirah atlantis.com · DDD

The original luxury Palm hotel has it all. More than 1,000 rooms, over 20 bars and restaurants (with multiple Michelin-starred spots), and two swimming pools. If this isn't enough, there is also the iconic water park, Aquaventure World *(p88)*, a bowling alley and a giant aquarium that seems to flow through the whole hotel.

Downtown Abu Dhabi

The Abu Dhabi Edition

N3 Marina Al Bateen W35 marriott.com · DD

This icon in Abu Dhabi combines all that you'd expect in a luxury hotel (elegant rooms and apartments, two pools, fitness centres and three restaurants) with more unique touches. There's the three-storey entertainment space, the unusual desert photography by Brett Weston and the one-of-a-kind "steak sommelier", who can help you find your perfect cut at the hotel's Oak Room restaurant.

Emirates Palace Mandarin Oriental

N1 West Corniche mandarinoriental.com · DDD

A stay at the Emirates Palace is a crash course in the good life. There are uniformed butlers to see to your every need and a fleet of limousines to whisk you around town. There is also the Emirates Palace Club to relax in, two Michelin-starred restaurants to eat in and the elegant Royal Afternoon Tea with treats covered in edible gold. It's little wonder many foreign dignitaries stay here.

Khalidiya Palace Rayhaan by Rotana

N2 Sir Bani Yas Island rotana.com · DD

In need of a family getaway? This relaxed resort, next to the Presidential Palace, might fit the bill. Aside from the private stretch of beach, the sports courts and large pool area, the hotel has its own kids' club, complete with a kids' pool and playground. Best of all, the club has a babysitting service, so parents can have some well-earned time alone.

Aloft Abu Dhabi

U3 ADNEC Centre Abu Dhabi marriott.com · D

Aloft Abu Dhabi may not be as luxury-orientated as other hotels, but it's a great option for those who wish to spend their days out and about. Its location close to the airport ensures a stress-free arrival and departure and local public transport options mean it's well connected to the city.

Beyond Abu Dhabi

St Regis Saadiyat Island Resort

Al Saadiyat Island marriott.com · DDD

Abu Dhabi has numerous oft-overlooked cultural attractions, many of which are minutes from the St Regis. The Zayed National Museum, Louvre Abu Dhabi, TeamLab Phenomena and Manarat Al Saadiyat gallery are all within walking distance of the hotel. But if you do want to relax, the St Regis is on the Arabian Sea and the beach is lovely.

W Abu Dhabi

W4 Yas Island marriott.com · DD

The world's only hotel that straddles an F1 track, the W Abu Dhabi gets you as close to the action as it can without putting you in the car itself. You can enjoy the thrill of the engines on the track or retreat to the private marina where you can recharge in a more tranquil setting. It's a treat for racing fans and non-racing fans alike.

Anantara Sir Bani Yas Island Al Sahel Villa Resort

Sir Bani Yas Island anantara.com · DDD

Escape the bustle of the city and reconnect with nature at this rural resort. The hotel is surrounded by lush savannah and fantastic wildlife, including cheetahs, giraffes, gazelles and the more local Arabian oryx, all of which can be spotted on the daily wildlife safaris. It's hard to believe you're not in Africa.

Telal Resort Al Ain

Remah Al Ain telalresort.ae/the-resort.html · DDD

Amid the mountainous dunes of the Remah Desert is this boutique hotel in a lush oasis. The Telal embraces its desert location through a wide variety of activities, from thrilling experiences like quad tours of the desert and archery lessons to cultural experiences, like traditional Emirati meals and tours of the nearby Zaman Lawal Heritage Village. You may even spot antelopes and oryx roaming the desert.

The Ritz-Carlton, Abu Dhabi Grand Canal

V4 Al Karamah Street ritzcarlton.com · DDD

You won't lack for space at this outpost of the Ritz-Carlton brand. The hotel is spread across 57 acres (23 hectares), which includes a private beach, palatial-sized rooms and suites, a vast spa and supposedly the largest pool in Abu Dhabi. The top floors have perhaps the single best view in the whole of the UAE, overlooking Sheikh Zayed Grand Mosque and the Al Maqta Creek.

INDEX

Page numbers in **bold** refer to main entries.

PHRASE BOOK

In an Emergency

Help!	*Enjedooni!*
Stop	*Wak-kaf*
Can you call a doctor?	*Momkin tatlob tabeeb?*
Can you call an ambulance?	*Momkin tatlob el es'aaf?*
Can you call the police?	*Momkin tatlob el shorta?*
Can you call the fire brigade?	*Momkin tatlob el etfaa?*
Where is the nearest hospital?	*Wayn agrab mostashfa?*
Is there a telephone here?	*Ako telefoon huna?*

Useful Words and Phrases

Yes	*Na-am*
No	*Laa*
Hello	*Salaam alaikum*
Goodbye	*Ma'aa al salaama*
See you later	*Ela al lekaa*
Excuse me	*'Afwan*
Sorry (said by man)	*Aasif*
Sorry (said by woman)	*Aasifa*
Thank you	*Shakereen*
Please	*Luw tasma`h*
Peace be upon you	*Al salaam 'alaikum*
Peace be upon you (as response)	*Alaikum al salaam*
Good morning	*Sabaa`h al khayr*
Good evening	*Masaa-o al khayr*
Good night	*Tosbihoona ala khayr*
Pleased to meet you	*Ya ahleen*
How are you?	*Keef al 'haal?*
I'm fine	*Zeen*
I don't understand	*Ma afham*
What did he say?	*Shenu kaal?*
Do you speak English?	*Ta'hki enkleezi?*
Does anyone speak English?	*Aku 'hada ye'hkee enkleezi?*
Have you got a table for…?	*Aku taawila hug …?*
I would like to reserve a table	*Areed a'hjiz taawila*
Can I have the bill please?	*Al 'hesaab luw tasma'h?*
I am vegetarian	*Ana nabaati*
God willing	*Inshaal-la*
big	*kabeer*
small	*sageer*
hot	*'haar*
cold	*baarid*
bad	*say-ye'e*
good	*tay-yeb*
open	*maftoo'h*
closed	*mesak-kar*
on the right	*'ala al yameen*
on the left	*'ala al yasaar*
near	*kareeb*
far	*ba'eed*
men's toilet	*twalet hug al rejaal*
ladies' toilet	*twalet hug al 'hareem*
a little	*kaleel*
a lot	*waajed*

Making a Telephone Call

Hello	*Aloo*
I'd like to speak to…	*Areed akal-lim…*
This is…	*Ana…*
I'll call back later	*Raa'h at-tasel ba'adeen*
Please say … called	*Khab-birho an-na… et-tasal*

In a Hotel

hotel	*fondok*
Do you have a room?	*Ladaykom 'hojra?*
I have a reservation	*Endi 'hajz*
With bathroom	*Bee 'ham-maam*
single room	*'hojra fardiy-ya*
double room	*'hojra le etneen*
porter	*natoor*
shower	*dosh*
key	*meftaa'h*

Sightseeing

art gallery	*ma'arad luw'haat faney-ya*
beach	*shaate'e*
bus station	*muwgaf el baahs*
district	*mentakaa*
entrance	*madkhal*
exit	*makhraj*
garden	*'hadeeka*
guide	*morshid*
guided tour	*morshid al juwla*
map	*khaarta*
mosque	*jaame'a*
museum	*mut'haf*
park	*motanaz-zah*
river	*naher*
taxi	*taksi*
ticket	*tathkara*
tourist office	*maktab seyaa'hi*
Please put the (taxi) meter on	*Luw tasma'h, daw-war al 'ad-daad*
How much is it to…?	*Kam raah tekal-lafni ela…?*
Please take me to (this address)	*Khothni ela (haaza al onwaan)*

Shopping

How much is it?	*Kam floos?*
I'd like…	*Areed*
This one	*Haaza*
Do you accept credit cards?	*Hal takbaloon kredit kaard?*
That's too much	*Haaza waayed*
I'll give you…	*Ana raa'h a'ateek…*
I'll take it	*Raa'h aakhdoh*
market	*sook*
expensive	*ghaali*
cheap	*rakhees*
chemist's	*saydalaani*

Menu Decoder

'aish	rice
'aseer	fruit juice
bedoon	without
bee	with
beera	beer
beez	egg
beez maslook	hard-boiled egg
beriaani al dajaaj	chicken biryani
beriaani al lahem	meat biryani
beriaani al robiaan	shrimp biryani
beriaani samak	fish biryani (with bones) spiced
bolti	tilapia (fish) grilled and served whole
da-en	mutton
dajaaj	chicken

faakiha	fruit
falaafel	vegetarian burger made with chickpeas
fee al forn	roasted
fulful	white pepper
fulful aswad	black pepper
gabgab	steamed crab
guhwa	bitter Arabic coffee
haleeb	milk
halwa	Turkish delight with cardamom
ham-moor	local fish that tastes like snapper
ham-moor magli	deep-fried hammoor
harees	gruel cooked in beef stock
heel	cardamom
holo	sweet
kabaab	kebab
kabsa	dish of rice, meat/chicken, dried lemon and saffron
kabsat dajaaj	dish of rice, chicken, dry lemon and saffron
kabsat lahem	dish of rice, meat, dry lemon and saffron
kereem	cream
khal	vinegar made from molasses
khamr	wine
khoboz	bread
khoboz jabaab	large spiced pancakes with cardamom
khoboz shaami	pita bread
khoboz tost	toast
kofta	grilled meatballs
koozi	lamb
koskos	plain couscous
maglee	fried
malh	salt
marag	spiced meat/ chicken stock
marag dajaaj	chicken stock
marag lahem	beef stock
mashroob ghaazi	soft drink
mashwi	grilled
mashwi ala el fa`hm	barbecued over coal
masloog	boiled
mohal-li senaa-ee	sweetener
moham-mas	toasted
nabeez	wine
neskafee	coffee
orz	rice
orz bil zafaraan	rice with saffron
robyaan	large grilled shrimp
shai	tea
shawirma	doner kebab
suk-kar	sugar
sulsa	tomato purée cooked in stock
tahye motawas-sit	medium
tshaaw meen dajaaj	chicken chowmein
tshaaw meen lahem	beef chowmein
tshaaw meen samak	seafood chowmein
tshoop sooy	chop suey
wajba khafeefa	snack
zaatar	thyme
zangabeel	ginger powder
zobod	butter

Numbers

1	waa'hid
2	etneen
3	thalaatha
4	arba'aa
5	khamsa
6	sit-ta
7	saba'a
8	thamaaneya
9	tes'aa
10	'ashra
11	'hedaash
12	etnaash
13	talat-taash
14	arba'-taash
15	khamastaash
16	sit-taash
17	saba'ataash
18	tamantaash
19	tesa'ataash
20	eshreen
21	waa'hid wa eshreen
30	thalatheen
40	arbe'een
50	khamseen
60	sit-teen
70	sab'een
80	thamaneen
90	tes'een
100	me-aa
1000	alf

Time

Today	el yoom
yesterday	el bariha
tomorrow	baaker
morning	sabaa'h
afternoon	zaheera
evening	masaa
night	lail
now	al 'heen
tonight	el laila
minute	dageega
hour	sa'aa
week	osboo'a
month	shahr
year	'aam

Days of the Week

Monday	al ethneen
Tuesday	al thulathaa
Wednesday	al arbe'a
Thursday	al khamees
Friday	al jomo'aa
Saturday	al sabet
Sunday	al a'had

Months

January	yanaayer
February	febraayer
March	maaris
April	abreel
May	maayo
June	yonyo
July	yolyo
August	agostos
September	sebtamber
October	oktoobar
November	noovambir
December	deesambir

ACKNOWLEDGMENTS

This edition updated by

Contributor Sarah Hedley Hymers

Senior Editors Keith Drew, Alison McGill

Senior Designers Katie Cavanagh, Vinita Venugopal

Project Editors Charlie Baker, Molly McCarthy

Project Art Editor Divyanshi Shreyaskar

Editors Catrina Conway, Nandini Desiraju, Sarah Mathew, Eleanora Reeves, Vineet Singh

Proofreader Kathryn Glendenning

Indexer Helen Peters

Deputy Picture Research Manager Virien Chopra

Rights and Permissions Specialist Priya Singh

Assistant Picture Research Administrator Manpreet Kaur

Publishing Assistant Simona Velikova

Jacket Designers Laura O'Brien, Divyanshi Shreyaskar

Jacket Picture Researcher Kate Hockenhull

Project Cartographer Ashif

Senior Cartographer James Macdonald

Cartography Manager Suresh Kumar

Pre-production Coordinator Tanveer Zaidi

Pre-production Designer Rajdeep Singh

Pre-production Image Coordinator Jagtar Singh

Pre-production Manager Balwant Singh

Image Retouching Production Manager Pankaj Sharma

Senior Production Controller Samantha Cross

Deputy Managing Editor Dharini Ganesh

Managing Editor Beverly Smart

Managing Art Editor Gemma Doyle

Senior Managing Art Editor Priyanka Thakur

Editorial Director Hollie Teague

Art Director Maxine Pedliham

Publishing Director Georgina Dee

DK would like to thank the following for their contribution to the previous editions: Lara Dunston, Sarah Monaghan, Gavin Thomas.

The publisher would like to thank the following for their kind permission to reproduce their photographs:

Key: a-above; b-below/bottom; c-center; f-far; l-left; r-right; t-top

123RF.com: bloodua 49b.

Adobe Stock: Gonzalo 46; Kertu 40cla; Rastislav Sedlak SK 13tl.

Alamy Stock Photo: Anna Stowe Travel 34bl; Art Directors & TRIP / Helene Rogers 9cr; Cristiano Barni 13bl; Yogi Black 9tl; Chronicle 8; eFesenko 35; Eibner-Pressefoto / Annika Graf 38; Every Second Media 10bl; Juergen Hasenkopf 27bl; Hauser Patrice / Hemis.fr 66; Image Professionals GmbH / LOOK-foto 15tl; IMAGO / ERZ-Foto / Georg Ulrich Dostmann 54b; Jon Arnold Images Ltd 70t; John Kellerman 27cb; Viacheslav Khmelnytskyi 88; Karol Kozlowski Premium RF 56–57; Art Kowalsky 72; LH Images 14crb; Frédéric Marie 33t; Iain Masterton 64t; mauritius images GmbH / Maria Breuer 34cb; Middle East 81; Old Books Images 9crb; Dimple Patel 34clb; Philippe Turpin / Photononstop 15clb; Quagga Media 9tr; Simon Reddy 50t; robertharding / Fraser Hall 43; Robin Weaver 14bc; Edward Webb 47; WorldTravel 71.

Armani Hotel: 22b.

Ashas: 73.

Atlantis, The Palm: 89.

Atlantis, The Palm – Aquaventure: 48–49t.

AWL Images: Jon Arnold 22–23t, 61; Cahir Davitt 1; Susanne Kremer 11; Stefano Politi Markovina 19; Chris Mouyiaris 13clb, 24–25b.

Bab Al Shams: 41t.

Burj Al Arab: 20c, 30cla, 30–31b, 31t, 80.

Courtesy of Mimi Kakushi: 52b.

Department of Culture and Tourism–Abu Dhabi: Hufton & Crow 44tl.

Dreamstime.com: Tamer Adel 10cl; Alexkane1977vi 87t; Altayebamer 55t; Cristian Andriana 58–59b; Michal Bednarek 87b; Carabiner 82b; Evgeniy Fesenko 16cr, 25t; Sergii Figurnyi 21br; Frantic00 16tl, 32–33b; Waqar Hussain 50b; Mohamad Kaddoura 51; Shahid Khan 76; Manowar1973 54t; Dmitrii Melnikov 13cl; Manoj Mundapat 58t; Franco Nadalin 27br; Outcast85 96; Nancy Pauwels 6–7; Bernadett Pogácsás-Simon 12cra; Saletomic 94–95; Santiaga 92; Stanislawrulinski 77; Alexey Stiop 12crb; TasFoto 55b; Tea 75; Aleksandra Tokarz 70b; Topdeq 99.

Dubai Creek Golf & Yacht Club: 63.

Getty Images: Moment Unreleased / Captured Blinks Photography 12cr; Stone / John Harper 82–83t; The Image Bank Unreleased / Atlantide Phototravel 13cl (8); Sidney-Barton / Keystone / Hulton Archive 10br; The Image Bank Unreleased / Peter Unger 12bl.

Getty Images / iStock: brunocoelhopt 39; E+ / Nikada 105; frantic00 10tl; Glen_Pearson 17t; Kabir Uddin 34br; undefined undefined 16tc.

Hakkasan Abu Dhabi: 17bl, 97.

Jumeirah Mosque: 28, 29t, 29b.

Karma Kafé: 79.

Madinat Jumeirah / Bahri Bar: 85.

Marriott International: Bar 44 52t; Siddharta Lounge by Buddha-Bar / Neil Corder 90.

One&Only Royal Mirage: Tagine 91.

Radisson Blu Hotel / The China Club: 67.

Shangri-La Qaryat Al Beri, Abu Dhabi: 103.

Sheikh Zayed Grand Mosque: 17bc, 21bl, 36–37t, 37br.

Shutterstock.com: Emad Aljumah 69; Erik Duarte 13cla; frantic00 93; Me.Karim1983 100–101; MikeDotta 64b; Rashid.5.5 40–41b; RiadSeif 21t; snaptheframe 5.

Souk Madinat Jumeirah: 84.

The Third Line: 44b.

Towers Rotana Dubai: Longs Bar 78.

XVA Gallery, Café & Hotel: Nathan Root 45.

Y Bar: 102.

Cover Images:

Front and Spine: **Sheikh Zayed Grand Mosque**; *Back:* **AWL Images:** Chris Mouyiaris cl; **Getty Images**: Stone / John Harper tr; **Shutterstock.com**: Erik Duarte tl.

Sheetmap Cover Image:

Sheikh Zayed Grand Mosque.

A NOTE FROM DK

The rate at which the world is changing is constantly keeping the DK travel team on our toes. While we've worked hard to ensure that this edition of Dubai and Abu Dhabi is accurate and up-to-date, we know that opening hours alter, standards shift, prices fluctuate, places close and new ones pop up in their stead. So, if you notice we've got something wrong or left something out, we want to hear about it. Please get in touch at travelguides@dk.com

Within each Top 10 list in this book, no hierarchy of quality or popularity is implied. All 10 are, in the editor's opinion, of roughly equal merit.

First edition 2007

Published in Great Britain by Dorling Kindersley Limited, DK, 20 Vauxhall Bridge Road, London SW1V 2SA

The authorised representative in the EEA is Dorling Kindersley Verlag GmbH. Arnulfstr. 124, 80636 Munich, Germany

Published in the United States by DK Publishing, 1745 Broadway, 20th Floor, New York, NY 10019, USA

25 26 27 28 10 9 8 7 6 5 4 3 2 1

A CIP catalog record for this book is available from the British Library.

A catalog record for this book is available from the Library of Congress.

ISSN: 1479-344X
ISBN: 978 0 2417 5755 0

Printed and bound in China

www.dk.com

This book was made with Forest Stewardship Council™ certified paper – one small step in DK's commitment to a sustainable future.

Learn more at **www.dk.com/uk/information/sustainability**